THE NEW LEADER

THE NEW LEADER

MYRON RUSH

VICTOR BOOKS®

A DIVISION OF SCRIPTURE PRESS PUBLICATIONS INC.
USA CANADA ENGLAND

Victor Books by Myron Rush:

BURNOUT
LORD OF THE MARKETPLACE
MANAGEMENT: A BIBLICAL APPROACH

Second printing, 1989

Unless otherwise noted, Scripture quotations are from the *Holy Bible, New International Version*, © 1973, 1978, 1984, International Bible Society. Used by permission of Zondervan Bible Publishers. Verses marked TLB are taken from *The Living Bible*, © 1971, Tyndale House Publishers, Wheaton, IL 60189. Used by permission.

Recommended Dewey Decimal Classification: 658.3
Suggested Subject Heading: LEADERSHIP

Library of Congress Catalog Card Number: 87-81026
ISBN: 0-89693-348-2

CONTENTS

The Need for a Revolutionary Approach to Leadership

Ever since I can remember, the Christian community has been complaining about the shortage of leaders in its ranks, and in recent years the complaints have turned into cries of alarm.

It is the opinion of this writer that we are headed for even greater leadership shortages in Christendom unless we redefine the functions and purpose of leadership. A shortage of leaders tends to produce a more serious leadership shortage. *A shortage of leaders creates a shortage of followers. And a shortage of followers produces a shortage of future leaders.*

The end result of this cycle of leadership shortages is obvious—an entire organization, society, nation, or worldwide movement can slowly be eliminated because of the diminishing number of effective leaders and followers needed to carry on its mission.

The shortage of leaders in the Christian community is already taking an alarming toll. Many of the once strong and growing mainline denominations are experiencing increasing declines in memberships. Some denominations are being forced to close church doors because there are not enough pastors available.

Bible schools and seminaries with long histories and traditions of service to the Christian community are closing because of the lack of students and financial support. Many Christian organizations are experiencing greater and greater difficulty finding qualified leaders to fill key positions. The head of a large mission organization recently told me, "It used to be that we had more people wanting to go to the mission field than we had slots available. However, now we have more slots available than qualified people."

A SHORTAGE OF LEADERS CREATES A SHORTAGE OF FOLLOWERS, AND A SHORTAGE OF FOLLOWERS PRODUCES A SHORTAGE OF FUTURE LEADERS.

Even local churches are feeling the effects of the ongoing leadership shortage. Many churches are complaining that they are having more and more difficulty finding qualified people to fill teaching positions, serve on committees, head various departments, and serve on the important boards within the church. Some churches are even being forced to sell their facilities to secular groups because there are no longer enough people to support them.

Unfortunately, while the leadership shortage is taking a serious toll within Christendom, atheistic Communism is sweeping the world like a tidal wave. Not since first-century Christianity has a movement engulfed the world as rapidly as Communism.

In less than a century the political forces of atheistic Communism have grasped control of over one third of the world's population. And if you were to count the various cults, groups, and movements—such as the multifaceted New Age movement—who strongly embrace most of the same humanistic and atheistic values as Communism, the figure would be much higher.

The question is why. The answer is frustrating and disgusting! Satan has stolen the New Testament approach to leadership and used it to promote his cause, while at the same time he has lulled the Christian community into apathy and sleep by selling them a watered-down version of leadership.

Satan never tries to sell the Christian a big lie. The Apostle Paul points out that "Satan himself masquerades as an angel of light" (2 Cor. 11:14). He tries to convince us that a half-truth is the whole truth and thereby deceive us. And that is exactly what he has accomplished among us.

He has led us to believe that as long as we apply some of the *elements* of leadership, we are leaders. He has convinced many of us that holding an important *position* of leadership is the same as being an effective leader. He has limited our ability to develop effective leaders in sufficient quantity by selling us a definition of leadership contrary to the example of leadership demonstrated by Jesus Christ in the New Testament.

In the pages of this book we will be examining a "new" approach to modern leadership. In reality it is not new—it was systematically practiced by Jesus Christ and the early church some two thousand years ago and is currently being very successfully used by the leaders of Communism today. However, for years we in the Christian community have been applying only bits and pieces of New Testament leadership; therefore, for many of us it is new today.

Compared to what we are used to it certainly is revolutionary! Jesus Christ was not content just to acquire followers. He didn't believe a leader was simply one who leads followers. He felt His job as a leader was not complete until He had actually reproduced Himself in the lives of His twelve disciples and turned them from followers into leaders. He actually redefined effective leadership.

The purpose of this book is to help you and me rediscover the practices and principles of leadership taught and applied by Jesus Christ some two thousand years ago. Some of you have already discovered those principles and are effectively applying them. For others, some of the points being made in this book may go beyond what you have traditionally considered to be the essentials of leadership.

Whether you agree with every point presented in this book or not, it is my prayer that God will use this text to sharpen your skills as a leader and make you more effective in accomplishing the job He has given you to do.

Myron D. Rush
President
Management Training Systems

CHAPTER ONE

The New Leader's Role

As stated in the introduction to this book, the Christian community is facing a serious leadership shortage—a shortage of such magnitude that it threatens the life of evangelical Christianity. A home, church, business, government, or society is only as healthy and strong as its leadership. The current success and future existence of the institutional church rest squarely on the shoulders of its leaders.

While attending graduate school at Central Missouri State University I took a course entitled Politics and Power. The instructor pointed out that natural resources represent a very important source of power for any nation or society. He went on to explain that we are slowly using up all of the natural resources of the world. Those nations that control the most resources will likely maintain their power longer.

We certainly are experiencing increasing shortages of resources in our society today. All of us were affected by the recent energy shortage. Many cities are currently suffering from serious water shortages. The shortage of clean air in our cities poses a severe health hazard for millions of people each day.

Soil conservation experts warn us that we are facing a serious shortage of the topsoil needed for growing food for the billions of people in the world today. They tell us that each year wind and water erosion carry off billions of tons of valuable topsoil, and eventually there won't be enough available to support life on this planet.

All of these shortages are certainly serious and pose severe problems for our society, but none is as serious as the shortage of leaders. We are in the midst of a leadership crisis in this country far more serious than the energy crisis or any other natural resource shortage.

And the leadership shortage among Christians is the most serious crisis of all. It is the godly influence of the Christian community that holds back the forces of evil in cities and nations. The shortage of strong, effective, godly Christian leaders is greatly weakening our ability to stand against the forces of Satan. The results will be devastating.

Notice what Proverbs 11:11 tells us. "The good influence of godly citizens causes a city to prosper, but the moral decay of the wicked drives it downhill" (TLB). And again in Proverbs 28:2 we are warned, "When there is moral rot within a nation, its government topples easily; but with honest, sensible leaders there is stability."

A nation full of godly people is far more powerful against the forces of evil in the world than all of the world's greatest weapons of war combined. That is why Satan has been working overtime trying to undermine the effectiveness of Christian leaders.

He knows that if he can reduce the number of Christian leaders and their effectiveness then he will also begin reducing the number of followers of Jesus Christ. And the fewer the number of Christians and the less effective their leaders, the easier it will be for him to take over and control the world.

God's Work Depends on Effective Leaders
The growth and spread of Christianity happen in proportion to the supply of effective leaders. Ted Grant is the pastor of a

large, dynamic, and rapidly growing church in the southwestern part of the country. However, when I first met Ted several years ago, the church was having numerous problems and struggling to maintain an average attendance of two hundred for the Sunday morning worship service. The church was also heavily in debt.

I first met Ted at a management seminar I was conducting for pastors and church leaders in his area. At that time Ted was a very frustrated pastor. Since he felt I was an outsider he could trust, he poured his heart out to me concerning the problems he was having getting qualified leaders in the church. He told me he was having difficulty recruiting Sunday School teachers, members for the missions committee, department heads, and board members.

During our conversation Ted had said, "It seems like I can't find anyone who wants to do anything but sit in the pew and watch while a handful of us do all the work. It's no wonder we have problems. You can't build a strong church without leaders!"

Last year I had the privilege of visiting Ted's church. It was a far cry from the one he had described several years earlier. They had just completed a new sanctuary and were planning a new educational wing. They had over three thousand people attending two morning worship services each Sunday. And their missions budget was almost a million dollars.

After the service I had an opportunity to have a long talk with Ted. I asked him what he felt the key to their growth had been. He smiled and replied, "About five years ago we started a leadership training program in our church. We taught people *how* to be leaders before expecting them to volunteer for a leadership role."

Ted explained that the leadership training program had accomplished what years of preaching had failed to achieve. "Once we started training our people how to lead, how to teach, and how to reproduce themselves in others, we had no problems finding qualified people to meet the leadership needs of the church."

With a bright gleam of success in his eyes he continued, "In fact, we have trained so many leaders in our church we have started a satellite church in order to put them all to work."

Listening to Ted Grant that day reminded me of the important role leaders play in the success of any organization. Without proper leadership Ted's church struggled to survive, but once they began to develop effective leaders, the church became a highly successful organization. Training effective leaders was the key to their success.

Ted's church clearly illustrates that the growth of Christianity is in direct proportion to the supply and availability of effective leaders.

The Purpose of This Book

This is not a book on the *theory* of leadership. It is hoped that you will find it to be a practical working manual on a new and effective way of leading people and turning followers into leaders like yourself.

There are application assignments at the end of each chapter. I trust you will study them carefully and apply them to your specific needs and situations, because you learn to lead by doing. The spectator on the sidelines or the person who is always content to faithfully "warm the pew" is only following the game, not leading the charge.

As you will see, this is much more than a book on how to lead followers. It is a book on how to turn followers into leaders. Therefore, the appendix of this book provides you with some tools for training others to become leaders like yourself (if you are already a leader). It shows you how to teach others the principles presented in each chapter. You haven't really completed the book until you have used the appendix to train others to be leaders.

My prayer is that this book will cause you to reevaluate your current leadership approach and that you will be willing to roll up your sleeves and begin the hard work of applying this new approach. If we want to follow Jesus Christ's example in our private lives, then shouldn't we also follow His example in our leadership?

Identifying the "New" Leader

What is a leader? For years we have said, "A leader is simply one who leads." One dictionary defines a leader as one who "guides by showing the way."

I would like to suggest that a leader is far *more* than that. Leadership as taught by Jesus Christ and practiced by the early church does not stop with leading the way. Satan doesn't want us to discover that. He wants the Christian leader to keep very busy leading the followers for two reasons: it keeps the leader constantly occupied, and it makes the followers totally dependent upon the leader.

In order to understand the "new" approach to leadership, we must take a close look at what Jesus Christ did as a leader. On the surface it might appear that He did what most other leaders do—lead His followers along the way that they should go—but that was not Jesus Christ's ultimate purpose as a leader.

In order to understand this new approach to leadership, we must first understand why Jesus Christ became a leader in the first place. He didn't have to if His sole purpose was to die for our sins. If Jesus' only job was to die on the cross in order to pay the penalty for our sins, He could have come to earth, quietly lived His life, and at the appointed time offered Himself as the sacrifice for the sins of mankind. However, we all know He didn't do that.

In addition to coming to earth to pay the price for our sins, Jesus had another equally important job. He also came to train leaders to take the good news of the Gospel to the "uttermost parts of the earth."

His ultimate purpose as a leader was not to lead His followers to the cross or simply show them by example how to live a godly life, though He did both of these. His main purpose was to develop leaders out of His followers.

That is why Jesus was so successful as a leader. That is also why the leaders of the first-century church were so successful in taking the Gospel to the known world. And that is why Communism is so successful today. The purpose of leadership as taught and demonstrated by Jesus Christ, carried on by the leaders of the early church, and then adopted from the New Testament by Communism, is to make leaders out of followers.

So, using Jesus Christ's life as an example and copying the principles of leadership taught and applied by Him and the early church leaders, we can redefine a leader as one who *recruits people to follow his example and guides them along the way while he is training them to do what he does.*

What is the difference between the traditional leader and the leader copying Jesus Christ's approach to leadership? Both leaders recruit people to follow their example. Both guide their followers along the way. Unfortunately, traditional leaders usually stop there. The most important tasks, however, still lie ahead of the leader, because the new leader's objective is to train followers to do what he or she does. Effective leaders learn how to reproduce themselves in others. Their purpose is to help followers become leaders like themselves.

WE MUST DEVELOP LEADERS WHO KNOW NOT ONLY HOW TO RECRUIT AND LEAD PEOPLE BUT ALSO HOW TO TURN FOLLOWERS INTO LEADERS.

Being in an important position of leadership is no sign that you are actually an effective leader. Many people hold very important positions of leadership and have quite impressive leadership titles. You may even be very effective in applying many of the elements and functions of leadership, such as recruiting followers and guiding them toward reaching goals.

Jesus Christ's position as Son of God did not automatically make Him an effective leader. He was an effective leader because He trained people to do what He did. In Luke 9:1-6 we see Jesus training His followers to do exactly what He did. He gave them power and authority over demons and told them to "preach the kingdom of God and to heal the sick." He also told them to "take nothing for the journey—no staff, no bag, no bread, no money, no extra tunic." He trained them not only to do what He did as their leader, but to live in the same way He lived.

I may get myself in hot water and alienate many readers by making the following statements, but someone needs to say it: there are many pastors, Sunday School teachers, choir directors, and church board members in positions of leadership who aren't really leaders but performers and entertainers. Countless thousands of people attend church every Sunday and watch Sunday School teachers, choir directors, and pastors perform for them. But the vast majority of those people never get out of their pews and follow the people in the positions of leadership and actually learn to do what they do. It is much easier to perform for people and entertain people than it is to lead people.

Have you ever noticed what happens to attendance in most churches when the pastor is out of town and someone else from the church has to fill in? All too often many people stay away from church because their leader won't be there. That is a sure sign that they are learning to be dependent on the leader and not actually learning to do what he does.

The tragedy is that many performers and entertainers think they are leaders because they are up in front of their audience working so hard. But as long as traditional leaders are content to let followers watch them perform and fail to get them involved in doing what they are doing, they will remain only performers—no matter how great their positions or titles are.

If you are a Sunday School teacher, how many people are following your example and becoming teachers like yourself because you are training them to do what you do? The answer to that question will tell you whether you are a performer for your class of followers or a leader like Jesus Christ.

THE GROWTH AND SPREAD OF CHRISTIANITY HAPPEN IN PROPORTION TO THE SUPPLY OF EFFECTIVE LEADERS.

If you are a pastor, how many people are following your example and are in the ministry today because you are working with them and showing them how to do what you are doing? The answer to that question will tell you if you are performing for an audience or leading people the way Jesus Christ led His disciples.

Setting the Example

One of the major roles of the effective leader is to set the right example and then train others how to follow it. The Apostle Paul was one of the early church's greatest leaders. In 1 Corinthians 11:1 he wrote, "And you should follow my example, just as I follow Christ's" (TLB). And again in Philippians 3:17 he said, "Dear brothers, pattern your lives after mine and notice who else lives up to my example" (TLB).

We have already seen that Jesus Christ focused on training His followers to do what He did. Paul was doing the same thing; he wanted his followers to learn to do what he was doing. He knew that was the key to effective leadership.

Leaders not only set the pace, they train their followers to keep up. At some point, they move aside. Jesus said, "I tell you the truth, anyone who has faith in Me will do what I have been doing. He will do even greater things than these, because I am going to the Father" (John 14:12).

Jesus not only trained people to do what He did; His goal was for them to do even greater things than He was doing. This is the true mark of an effective leader. Your job isn't just to train people to do what you do, but to encourage them to do it even better!

Why We Don't Want to Set the Example

During this century Communism—working right under the nose of Christianity—has taken over almost one third of the population of the world. In the last few decades the efforts of atheistic Communism have successfully turned much of the world's opinion against the United States, which for years was the major exporter of Christianity around the world. In terms of reaching the hearts and minds of people, Communism is succeeding where the Christian church is failing.

HOLDING AN IMPORTANT POSITION OF LEADERSHIP IS NO SIGN THAT YOU ARE AN EFFECTIVE LEADER.

Why is that happening? Communism, using the New Testament principles of leadership taught and practiced by Jesus Christ, has stepped forward and shown the Christian church how to recruit followers and train them as leaders in promoting their cause.

On the other hand, Christians are complaining about our lack of leaders, but we are reluctant to set the example and then train people to do what we do. Why?

We do not understand the true meaning of humility. Many Christians feel there is a conflict between setting an example of humility and setting an example for others to follow. Some people feel you can't be a humble person and a strong leader at the same time.

That is exactly what Satan wants you to think. He wants you to believe that Christians are to keep quiet, hide out in the woods somewhere, and never draw attention to themselves. But Jesus Christ lived on the cutting edge of society. He confronted the religious leaders of the day. He mingled with the poor and the sinners on the street. And He always stood up for what He believed and was committed to training others to do what He did. He also said, "Take My yoke upon you and learn from Me, for I am gentle and humble in heart, and you will find rest for your souls" (Matt. 11:29).

If we are going to be effective leaders, we must understand the true meaning of humility. Humble persons don't boast about their achievements or abilities, but that doesn't mean they're not high achievers.

When Paul wrote to the Corinthians that they should follow his example as he followed Christ's, he was giving all the credit to Jesus Christ, not bragging. If you want to be an effective leader you must develop an attitude like Paul's. Step forward and challenge people to follow your example and then give the credit for the results to Jesus Christ.

We are afraid of what others might think or say. Paul did not try to please people; his goal was to please God. "We are not trying to please men but God, who tests our hearts" (1 Thes. 2:4). When you fail to step forward and become an open example for others to follow because you are afraid of what others might think or say, you are more interested in pleasing men than God, and you will never become an effective leader that way.

Don't worry about being criticized—there will always be someone who doesn't agree with what you are doing or how you are doing it. If you don't think so, look at how Jesus Christ was criticized—and His greatest critics came from within the religious community. It's always better to be criticized by people for doing something than to be criticized by God for doing nothing!

We are afraid of making mistakes. The fear of making a mistake causes many people to slide further down into their easy chairs and not step forward to become an example for others to follow.

When Carl McCutchan shared the Gospel with me during a Bible study several years ago, that same week he challenged me to start a Bible study with someone else. In astonishment I replied, "But Carl, I don't know how to lead a Bible study! What if they ask me questions I can't answer?"

Carl had a simple answer. "Just tell them you don't know the answer, but you'll find it for them and that way you'll both learn something."

I shook my head and replied, "But what if I make a big mistake and blow it bad?"

I'll never forget Carl's answer. He looked me straight in the eye and said, "Myron, the only big mistake you can make is not trying. Sure, you'll blow it occasionally. But no failure can ever be as bad as the failure to try."

I have never forgotten Carl's statement. *No failure can ever be as bad as the failure to try!* Never be afraid to try.

People become effective leaders because of what they learn along the way, not because of what they knew when they started out.

Great obstacles make strong leaders. And when you make a mistake, you have won a victory—you just discovered something you didn't know. A mistake is nothing more than a great opportunity to learn.

We don't feel qualified. Many people don't want to set an example for others to follow because they don't feel qualified. But it has been my experience that the people who feel the most qualified frequently make the poorest examples to follow.

If you don't feel qualified to be an example for others to follow, you have great leadership potential. On the other hand, if you feel that you have all—or at least most—of the answers and that you are the most qualified in your group to lead them, you will probably make a very poor leader.

Moses is one of my favorite people in the Bible. I have learned a lot about management and leadership by studying the life of Moses.

I think most of us would agree that he became one of the great leaders of the Old Testament. Notice Moses' reaction when God first asked him to lead the Children of Israel out of Egypt. "But I'm not the person for a job like that!" (Ex. 3:11, TLB)

Every time I read that verse, I laugh. Moses not only thought he wasn't qualified for the job, he must have thought God was not qualified to pick the right person for the job. Moses was actually telling God He had made a mistake in choosing him for the leadership job. The audacity of Moses!

Yet we frequently do the same thing. We try to tell God we aren't qualified to be examples for others to follow.

Don't you think God knows we aren't qualified? That is why He uses us. That is why He sent His Son to die on the cross for our sins. Of course we aren't qualified! We are all reprobates—wicked sinners saved by grace. If you are waiting until you are qualified before you volunteer to be an example for others, Satan will see to it that you never feel good enough to be a leader.

Paul realized this when he wrote, "Brothers, think of what you were when you were called. Not many of you were wise by human standards; not many were influential; not many were of noble birth. But God chose the foolish things of the world to shame the wise" (1 Cor. 1:26-27).

When Jesus called the twelve disciples to follow Him and become the future leaders of the early church, not one of them was a seminary graduate who had taken courses in homiletics, ecclesiology, or hermeneutics. They were common people ranging from commercial fishermen to the equivalent of IRS employees. They were just people like you and me, yet they became the great leaders of the New Testament.

God wants to use you in a new way. He wants you to take a close look at the life of Jesus Christ and not only tell others what you see but begin doing what He did—train your followers to be leaders like yourself!

Chapter Summary

We live in a world of shortages. But the greatest shortage of all is the shortage of Christian leaders who are willing to throw off the traditional approach to leadership and become leaders of a new and different kind—leaders not only willing to recruit followers, but like Jesus Christ, to train followers to do what they do.

Personal Application

1. What is the difference between the traditional approach to leadership and the "new" approach described in this chapter?
2. What should you be doing to begin effectively applying the new definition of a leader in your life?
3. Evaluate the leadership needs in the following areas:
   - Your home
   - Your church
   - Your job or business
   - Other organizations, clubs, or committees
4. How could applying the new approach to leadership better meet those needs?
5. What specific actions will you take in each of the areas listed in question three in order to begin applying the new approach to leadership?

CHAPTER TWO

Qualities of an Effective Leader

Four men have had a major influence in my life thus far: Carl McCutchan, the man who led me to Christ and spent three years of his life training me to study and apply the Bible to my life and to share what I had learned with others; Rush Johnston, a close friend for the past fifteen years who trained me in the principles of living by faith; Jerry Marshall, a great friend and former business partner who taught me many biblical principles of management; and Jim Ander, a former business partner and great personal friend who stuck by me and continued to believe in me during the most trying times and bitter experiences of my life and taught me how to keep balance in my life.

All of these men have one thing in common. They are effective leaders in their own areas of influence. What made them so effective? It wasn't simply their knowledge of their subjects and areas of expertise or their ability to set an example for others to follow. It was their ability to train me to do what they did. I now do many of the same things they do. In many ways I have become what they are. That is the real goal of leadership.

For the past sixteen years I have been deeply involved in the development of managers as leaders. Because I have worked in both private industry and government agencies, developed and operated several businesses, and worked as a management consultant, I have had the opportunity to observe hundreds of leaders in action.

In order to apply New Testament principles of leadership, we must pattern our lives after the model of Jesus Christ. We must learn to lead people the way He led people. We must do the things He did and develop the leadership qualities He displayed.

Christ possessed six very important qualities, which made Him the greatest leader the world has ever seen. We need to take a close look at those qualities, because new leaders must incorporate them into their lives if they want to follow Christ's example.

I should point out that traditional leaders possess the first four of these six qualities. However, the most important qualities are the last two. Here are the six:

- Effective leaders care about people.
- Effective leaders have strong personal convictions that guide their lives.
- Effective leaders are able to recruit people to their causes.
- Effective leaders challenge people to do their best.
- Effective leaders know how to train people to do what they do.
- Effective leaders know when to cut the cord and let people lead on their own.

Effective Leaders Care about People

Leaders are in the people business. Leaders who desire to lead according to biblical principles love people and care about them.

There are two kinds of leaders. Those of one kind try to use people for their own selfish purposes. Those of the other kind use purposes to meet the needs of people.

Leaders who use people for their own selfish gains see

people as nothing more than tools to accomplish their purpose of being the leader. In these leaders' view, people are expendable; these leaders have no real concern for the needs of individuals. Making sure they remain leaders is more important than anything else.

Such leaders usually lead by intimidating followers. I recently had a very embarrassing experience in which I observed this type of leader in action. I had been conducting a management seminar in Kansas City, and I was invited by a young business owner attending the seminar to go to church with him and his family the next day and then have dinner with them in his home before I had to catch a plane late Sunday afternoon for another speaking engagement.

I get tired of eating in restaurants when I travel, so I eagerly accepted the invitation. (I don't recall the people's name; I'll call them Mr. and Mrs. Jones.)

Sunday morning Mr. and Mrs. Jones picked me up at my hotel. And as I started to get in the backseat of their car with their son, Mr. Jones said, "No, no, Myron, you sit up here in the front seat with me. My wife can get in the backseat with Johnny."

I tried to explain that I would be perfectly comfortable in the backseat, but Mr. Jones insisted that his wife join their son and I sit in the front seat with him.

As we started off to church Mr. Jones assured me I would enjoy the service. He explained that their pastor was preaching a series of sermons on the home. All the way to the church he expounded on how important it is for the husband to assume his rightful place as leader of the family.

I don't remember much about the message. By the time we got to the church I was getting so angry with the way Mr. Jones was treating his wife that I regretted agreeing to go with them. I was convinced that no home-cooked meal could be worth watching Mr. Jones belittle his wife in front of a stranger.

All the way to church he picked on her. Every time she made a statement, he either disagreed or tried to correct what she said. After the service he scolded her for talking too long with her friends. When we got to their home, he criticized her for leaving the Sunday newspaper in a mess on the floor. Even though she had prepared a great meal with a wonderful dessert, he picked it apart. All the time he was picking on his wife and putting her down, he kept expounding on the need for more husbands to become strong leaders in their homes.

As I sat in the airport that afternoon waiting to catch my plane, I felt sorry for both Mr. and Mrs. Jones. I ached for her for having to put up with such a slob, and I felt sorry for him because he felt he had to intimidate her in order to be the leader of his home. He was obviously in charge, but he certainly didn't seem to care about the people he was leading. His only concern was to make sure his family recognized him as the leader and that they followed his instructions.

I often think about the Joneses and wonder just how long their marriage will last.

BLOWING OUT YOUR FOLLOWERS' CANDLES WON'T MAKE YOURS ANY BRIGHTER. BUT AS YOU USE YOURS TO LIGHT THEIRS, YOU NOT ONLY PROVIDE LIGHT FOR THEM, BUT MULTIPLY THE LIGHT OF YOUR OWN CANDLE MANY TIMES OVER.

The Bible points out that the leader is to care about people in the same way a shepherd cares about his flock. Notice what 1 Peter 5:2-3 tells us: "Feed the flock of God; care for it willingly, not grudgingly; not for what you will get out of it, but because you are eager to serve the Lord. Don't be tyrants, but lead them by your good example" (TLB).

Every leader should memorize this passage. It points out that we are to care for those we lead; we are not to use people and our leadership positions for our own personal glory; we are not to be tyrants; and we are to lead by good example.

Jesus faithfully cared for people. Notice His care for the people of Jerusalem: "O Jerusalem, Jerusalem. . . . How often I have wanted to gather your children together as a hen gathers her chicks beneath her wings, but you wouldn't let Me" (Matt. 23:37, TLB).

Many who think they want to be leaders actually want to be taskmasters. A taskmaster sits in an easy chair in the shade sipping a glass of pink lemonade, cracks a whip, and yells orders to his slaves. The servants take orders but are not allowed to do what he is doing.

It is much easier to be a taskmaster than a leader. The traditional leader gets out of his chair and steps into the hot, boiling sun, and rolling up his sleeves says, "Come on over here, folks. I'll do it for you, so you can see how it's done." The new leader gets out of his chair and steps into the hot, boiling sun, and rolling up his sleeves, says, "Come on, folks. I'll teach you how to do it and help you until we are done."

Both leaders care about the people. Both get out of their chairs and become examples for the followers. However, the traditional leader has been taught to demonstrate care by being an example. This leader may be the perfect example of how to do it right, but he or she winds up having to continuously be out front demonstrating how it is done.

On the other hand, new leaders not only set the example but train followers to do it the way they do it. They continue to help and care for followers until they have learned to become what the leaders are. At some point the followers will also become leaders.

Caring about people sometimes causes traditional leaders to step forward and do the job for the followers. On the other hand, caring about people motivates New Testament leaders to train followers to do what they do, so more people's needs can be met and the purpose is accomplished more quickly and easily.

As we think of the leader's role in caring for people, we must remember: blowing out your followers' candles won't make yours any brighter. But as you use yours to light those of your followers, you not only provide light for them, but multiply the light of your own candle many times over.

Effective Leaders Have Strong Personal Convictions

One of the ways leaders influence others is by having strong personal convictions. It was the strong personal convictions of the four men I mentioned earlier that first attracted me to them and later motivated me to learn from them.

A conviction can be defined as a fixed belief. Our convictions are the guiding force in directing our lives and influencing our decisions. Convictions are the foundation on which we build our lives. The stronger your convictions are, the stronger you are. You will never be a strong leader unless you first develop strong convictions.

Strong convictions remove doubt from your life. A strong leader is not a doubter. He is a very positive person. He is positive because he has strong convictions and those convictions help remove doubt.

And if you want to be an effective leader you can't be a doubter. Notice what James writes: "a doubtful mind will be as unsettled as a wave on the sea that is driven and tossed by the wind; and every decision you then make will be uncertain, as you turn first this way, and then that" (James 1:6-8, TLB).

Doubtful leaders get nowhere. People soon weary themselves trying to follow doubtful leaders. They don't know where they're headed, and their followers are right behind them in mass confusion.

If you are a leader experiencing lots of doubts, your convictions are not strong enough. Develop stronger convictions, and you will have fewer doubts.

Strong convictions help motivate you to action. Strong convictions help motivate leaders to become examples for others to follow. Our convictions are the sparks that ignite us into action.

When Carl McCutchan led me to Christ, he was willing to make time in his very busy schedule to teach me how to have a quiet time. He said, "Myron, if you are going to grow as a Christian, you must learn how to have a consistent, daily quiet time."

His convictions about that were so strong that he was willing to get up before 5 o'clock each morning for months to teach me how to have a consistent quiet time. We met at 5:00 in the morning because that was the only time we could find that our schedules permitted both of us to meet. Had Carl not had such strong convictions about the importance of learning to have a quiet time, he would not have been willing to get up before 5:00 in the morning to meet with me.

Strong personal convictions help turn followers into strong effective leaders.

Strong convictions help develop strong commitments. Recently I read of a young Communist terrorist who loaded his car with explosives, drove it into a building filled with people, and blew himself and his car up, killing several people in the process. That young man was highly committed to his cause, so committed that he was willing to give his life for it.

How strong are your convictions as a leader? How committed are you to promoting the cause of Jesus Christ? Are you committed enough to begin following New Testament principles of leadership?

Do you really believe there is a leadership shortage within the Christian community? If so, what are you doing to help reduce that shortage? As a leader are you willing to train others to do what you do?

One of the reasons Communism is sweeping the world is because its leaders have strong convictions. That is why they are willing to pay any price to achieve their goal. If we in the Christian community expect to reach the world with the

Gospel, our leaders must develop equally strong convictions.

Effective Leaders Are Able to Recruit People

Every good leader is also a good recruiter. The strong personal convictions that ignite leaders to action also motivate them to recruit others to follow their example.

If you want to measure people's leadership skills, look at the number of people they have trained to do what they are doing. Some people can fill an auditorium with listeners or watchers, but the true test of leadership is the number of people they train to follow their example.

New Testament leaders have the ability to recruit people, but being able to recruit people does not necessarily make you a New Testament leader, since traditional leaders can also recruit people to a cause. But they don't necessarily believe it is their job to train the followers to do what they do. Traditional leaders are satisfied if followers are willing to accept the philosophies of the cause and continue to support the leaders.

I have a friend who has been pastoring churches for over thirty years. He has great ability to draw people to listen to him because he has a very good personality and is an entertaining Bible teacher. However, he has constant trouble recruiting leaders in his church. It is one thing to be able to draw a crowd; it takes a real leader to be able to recruit people to a cause and train them for action to meet the ever-increasing needs of a growing church.

If I had an important job to accomplish, I would much rather give it to a leader who knows how to train followers to do what he does than to an entertainer whose followers have only been trained to listen.

Effective Leaders Challenge People to Do Their Best

Effective leaders not only perform well themselves; they also know how to help followers reach their full potential. The leader's role isn't simply to run ahead of followers as most traditional leaders do. The goal is performance reproduction.

If you want to help people perform at their best, never put limits on achievement. One of the reasons Jesus was such an effective leader is that He never put limits on what His followers could achieve. He said to them, "In solemn truth I tell you, anyone believing in Me shall do the same miracles I have done, and even greater ones, because I am going to be with the Father. You can ask Him for *anything*, using My name, and I will do it" (John 14:12-13, TLB).

No wonder the twelve disciples who followed Jesus became such great leaders. He never put limits on what they could achieve. And He makes that same promise to us and those following us!

One of the ways you can tell the difference between traditional leaders and New Testament leaders is that traditional leaders tend to encourage people to stay behind them and let them lead the way. New Testament leaders encourage followers to learn to do what they do, and then they challenge them to improve on their methods.

Effective Leaders Train People to Do What They Do

At this point the traditional leader and the New Testament leader part company. Most traditional leaders see themselves more as teachers than trainers. Teachers impart information and facts. Trainers also impart information and facts, but they then go the next step and train people to put the information into action.

If Jesus Christ had operated like many traditional leaders, the early church would not have gotten off the ground, because when His followers became the leaders, they would have stood around waiting for someone to train them.

Several years ago I hired Dale Letterman as a salesman for our company. Dale was an excellent salesman; the first year Dale worked for us, he broke all of our old sales records.

When we opened a branch office in Denver, we asked Dale

to be the sales manager there, but we quickly learned that we had made a major mistake. Dale knew how to sell our products better than any other salesperson in the company, but he couldn't train new people to sell. Before long we had to put Dale back in the field selling. He was an excellent performer, but a terrible leader.

IF YOU WANT TO KNOW HOW GOOD A PERSON'S LEADERSHIP SKILLS ARE, LOOK AT THE NUMBER OF PEOPLE HE HAS TRAINED TO DO WHAT HE IS DOING.

One of the major mistakes we make is to assume that a good performer will automatically make an excellent leader. Being able to perform well is no guarantee a person will be a good leader.

Unfortunately, we have a lot of people in the Christian community like Dale. They are good performers, so we promote them to positions of leadership. However, they aren't able to train others to do what they do, because their leaders were not trainers either.

But the difference between Dale and many of those people in leadership positions is that no one ever sits down with them and says, "You are a good performer, but you must also learn how to train people to do what you do." That is one of the reasons we have such a leadership shortage in the Christian community today.

Effective Leaders Know When to Cut the Cord

If we work to train our followers to do what we do, someday they will cease following us and begin to lead a group of followers of their own.

Turning our followers loose is easier said than done. They become our friends. We learn to rely on them and their abilities. We have put a lot of time and effort into training them, and if we let them go we will have to start all over with new recruits. All of these factors cause some leaders to be reluctant to turn their followers loose and let them come into their own as leaders.

Chapter Summary

The traditional leader and the New Testament leader possess many of the same qualities. However, the emphasis is not always the same, and the New Testament leader possesses two very critical qualities the traditional leader does not possess.

Both the traditional leader and the New Testament leader care about people, have strong personal convictions that guide their lives, have the ability to recruit people to a cause, and challenge people to perform at their best.

However, New Testament leaders also know how to train people to do what they do and they know when to cut the cord and let people lead on their own.

Personal Application

1. Review the qualities of a New Testament leader outlined in this chapter. How many of these qualities do you have? Which are your strongest ones? Which are your weakest ones?
2. What are you doing to demonstrate to your followers that you really care about them? What could you be doing that you are not?
3. Make a list of your personal convictions. How do they contribute to your ability to lead others? Which convictions need to be stronger?
4. What could you be doing to more effectively recruit people who will be willing to let you train them to do

what you do?

5. Evaluate your ability to train your followers to do what you are doing. What are your strengths and weaknesses as a trainer? What could you be doing to become a better trainer?

6. What are some things you should be doing to more effectively challenge your followers to perform their best? How are you communicating to them that you believe in them?

7. Do you have followers that you feel are ready to start leading others? If so, how do you plan to help them begin? If not, what do you plan to do to prepare them to lead others?

CHAPTER THREE

Paying the Price to Become an Effective Leader

Salvation is the only thing in life that is free. Everything else has a price, and the price tag on leadership is very high. That is one of the reasons we have such a shortage of leaders in this country today.

A lot of people want to be leaders. Most people seek the *positions* of leadership. However, very few people are willing to pay the price to become effective leaders.

It takes time to become an effective leader. Good leaders aren't developed in a day. You don't learn to be an effective leader sitting in a classroom. Being able to expound on the various theories and principles of leadership does not make you a good leader. Dressing like a leader has nothing to do with being a good leader.

When I graduated from high school I looked for a summer job to help pay my college expenses. I saw an ad in the newspaper for people to work for a contractor building houses. There were positions available ranging from laborer to foreman.

I applied for a position as a framer, but the owner said that I would have to start as a laborer unloading lumber off trucks because I didn't have any experience as a carpenter. He said, "Once you've learned the different sizes of boards, how to operate a tape measure, and get familiar with how we build houses, we'll eventually start working you into a framer's job."

But I wanted to start as a framer. I wanted to actually pound the nails and help build the house; I didn't want to be stuck unloading trucks and carrying boards to the people who were doing the *real* job. Since I couldn't have what I considered to be a real job, I didn't take any. I turned the laborer's job down and went to work in a grocery store stocking shelves and sacking groceries.

I didn't realize it at the time, but I had a serious problem— a problem that took years for me to overcome. I wasn't willing to pay the price of being a follower before I became a leader. I wanted to build the house, but I wasn't willing to take the time to learn the difference between a four-by-eight stud and a floor joist. It took several years before I learned the importance of investing the time and energy necessary in becoming a good follower so that at some point I could be an effective leader.

When Jesus Christ recruited the twelve disciples, He said, "Come, follow Me . . . and I *will make you* fishers of men" (Matt. 4:19, emphasis mine). He didn't say, "Come, follow Me, and you will automatically become fishers of men." The disciples had to be willing to invest time and energy as followers of Jesus Christ in order to become fishers of men.

Many of the Twelve had been commercial fishermen before becoming followers of Jesus Christ. They were professionals. They made their living fishing. They were probably part of the leadership of the local business community.

However, in order to learn how to fish for men they had to take a few steps down and become followers again before they would become qualified as leaders in God's business. This is a very important principle when it comes to developing spiritual leaders.

We must keep in mind that no matter what a person has accomplished as a leader in the secular world, he will still need to humble himself and invest the time and energy required to become a spiritual leader in God's business. There are no shortcuts to developing leadership skills.

In addition to time and energy, there are other prices that must be paid.

- You must be willing to stand alone.
- You must be willing to go against public opinion in order to promote what you believe.
- You must be willing to risk failure.
- You must become a master of your emotions.
- You must strive to remain above reproach.
- You must be willing to make decisions others don't want to make.
- You must be willing to say no at times, even when you'd like to say yes.
- You must sometimes be willing to sacrifice personal interests for the good of the group.
- You must never be content with the average; you must always strive for the best.
- People must be more important to you than possessions.
- You will have to work harder to keep your life in balance than people do who are not leaders.

Are you still interested in becoming an effective leader? If not, don't waste your time reading further. Please give this book to someone who is, and then ask your tax accountant if you can get a write-off for the donation! If you are still interested in becoming an effective leader, I can assure you that the returns on your investment will be more than worth the price you pay.

Standing Alone
Many people look at what they perceive to be the glamour of leadership and decide they want to be leaders. Some even decide they are called to be leaders. They want the respect or the power associated with positions of leadership. However, not all of those people realize the tremendous responsi-

bility that goes along with being a leader.

At this point I should point out that the Bible makes it very clear that it is good to aspire to positions of leadership. Notice Paul wrote to Timothy: "Here is a trustworthy saying: If anyone sets his heart on being an overseer, he desires a noble task" (1 Tim. 3:1). God certainly is pleased when people aspire to positions of leadership. However, He also wants us to count the cost involved. The Lord said, "Don't begin until you count the cost" (Luke 14:28, TLB).

One of the costs you must consider is your willingness to stand alone. As a leader there are times when you are the only one fighting for the cause. Even when no one else is willing to step forward, the leader always does. This is one of the great costs of leadership, and it is also one of the identifying marks of a leader.

When the Israelites assembled at the Valley of Elah to fight against the Philistines, no one in the army, including King Saul, was willing to step out to fight against the Philistines' giant, Goliath. When David, the young shepherd boy, arrived in the Israelite camp with food from home for his brothers and saw the situation, he went to King Saul and said, "Let no one lose heart on account of this Philistine; your servant will go and fight him" (1 Sam. 17:32).

David was willing to fight Goliath when no one else was. There will be times when you, like David, will have to step forward in a situation and say, "Let no one lose heart—I will do it!" That is the price you sometimes pay for being a leader. Sometimes you are required to stand alone for the sake of the cause.

Going against Public Opinion

Not only does the effective leader have to volunteer to stand alone at times for his cause, he must be prepared to stand against public opinion in order to promote what he believes. This is one of the highest prices a person has to pay in order to be an effective leader.

It's not easy to withstand the onrushing tide of public opinion when it is against you, but there are times when it is necessary. Notice Joshua's statement to the Children of Israel in Joshua 24:15: "But if serving the Lord seems undesirable to you, then choose for yourselves this day whom you will serve, whether the gods your forefathers served beyond the River, or the gods of the Amorites, in whose land you are living. But as for me and my household, we will serve the Lord."

Joshua wasn't a leader simply because he was the head of a nation; he was a leader because he was willing to pay the price. He was willing to go against public opinion in order to stand by and promote what he believed in.

What about you—are you willing to stick by your convictions even when popular opinion is against you? Or are you more interested in winning a popularity contest?

If you think being a good leader means winning popularity contests, you will never make it as a leader. The old saying "You can please some of the people some of the time, but you can't please all of the people all of the time" certainly applies to leadership.

There are times when you may not be able to please any of the people, but it's the entertainer's job to please all of the people all of the time. The leader's job is to set the right example and then challenge people to follow it. And if the right example isn't popular, then, like Joshua, you may have to stand against public opinion. It's the price the leader pays.

Risking Failure

Failure has different consequences for different people. For example, you expect your followers to fail occasionally, but your followers never expect you to fail. Leaders are under constant pressure to succeed. They're expected to always be out in front on the firing line. People don't think they will ever fail under the pressures of leadership. (And if they ever do, they don't know how to handle them or their failure.)

But all human beings fail—even great leaders!

IF LEADERS NEVER FAILED, WHO COULD EVER FOLLOW THEIR EXAMPLE?

Abraham failed (Gen. 12:10-13; 16:1-6). Moses failed (Ex. 2:11-12; Num. 11:10-23). David failed (2 Sam. 11:1-21). Peter failed (Matt. 26:69-75). And you and I fail.

The mark of a good leader isn't the absence of failure. The true test of leadership is how one handles failure. The great leaders from the Bible listed above failed. But they learned from their failures, and God continued to use them as effective leaders.

There is always risk in leadership. The leader encounters the possibility of failure far more often than his followers do, and the results are far more devastating when a leader fails than when a follower fails. That is just one of the prices we pay for being leaders.

Mastering Your Emotions
Effective leaders keep their emotions under control. No matter how they feel, good leaders strive to be guided by facts and principles.

When we allow our emotions to control us, we become much more susceptible to making errors in judgment and even becoming involved in serious failures. "A wise man controls his temper. He knows that anger causes mistakes" (Prov. 14:29, TLB). "*Above all else, guard your affections. For they influence everything else in your life*" (Prov. 4:23, TLB).

If you look at what caused Abraham, Moses, David, and Peter to fail, you will find that in each instance they allowed their emotions to control their decisions and they wound up deciding to act in a manner they knew was wrong. Had they been in better control of their emotions, none of them would have done what they did to bring on their failures.

When we allow our emotions to control us we are not only more prone to making mistakes, but we are also sure to say things we will regret later. This point is clearly illustrated in James 3:2-5. "If anyone can control his tongue, it proves that he has perfect control over himself in every other way. We can make a large horse turn around and go wherever we want by means of a small bit in his mouth. And a tiny rudder makes a huge ship turn wherever the pilot wants it to go, even though the winds are strong. So also the tongue is a small thing, but what enormous damage it can do" (TLB).

The more control we have over our emotions, the more we are in control of our tongues. And the more we control our tongues, the less trouble we make for ourselves and those around us.

Everyone should maintain self-control. However, it is even more important for leaders, because the actions and reactions of leaders not only affect themselves, but their followers as well. One of the prices we must pay as leaders is that of controlling our emotions—whether we feel like it or not. That is the only way we can maintain our effectiveness as leaders.

Remaining above Reproach

Just as effective leaders work to keep their emotions under control, they also strive to remain above reproach: "Now the overseer must be above reproach, the husband of but one wife, temperate, self-controlled, respectable, hospitable, able to teach, not given to much wine, not violent but gentle, not quarrelsome, not a lover of money.... He must also have a good reputation with outsiders, so that he will not fall into disgrace and into the devil's trap" (1 Tim. 3:2-3, 7).

What an excellent description of the character of a leader! I guess it should be—it came from the Bible, and God certainly knows the type of character one needs to be an effective leader.

THE RETURN ON YOUR INVESTMENTS FAR OUTWEIGHS THE COST OF BECOMING A LEADER.

Leading an exemplary life is one of the prices of effective leadership. There are things leaders can't do that other people can. Leaders must try to avoid any situation that might provide an opportunity for people to "talk."

Paul explains this point very well in Titus 2:7-8. "In everything set them an example by doing what is good. In your teaching show integrity, seriousness and soundness of speech that cannot be condemned, so that those who oppose you may be ashamed because they have nothing bad to say about us."

Recently I was out washing my car on a Sunday afternoon. I see nothing wrong with washing your car on Sunday. I have done it for years. However, a friend of mine happened to drive by my house and saw me washing my car on a Sunday afternoon. The next day she called me and in a very hurt and frustrated voice said, "Mr. Rush, I'm so disappointed in you. Don't you know it's wrong to work on Sunday? A person in your position should never wash his car on the Lord's Day. Why, what will people think?"

I had supposed they would think I didn't like driving a dirty car. But I had offended my friend, so now I try to wash my car on Saturday, Monday, Wednesday—I don't care, any day but Sunday!

Now, I still don't think it's wrong to wash my car on Sunday. But as a leader, I try to avoid doing things that offend others, especially Christians. Paul addresses this issue in 1 Corinthians: " 'Everything is permissible'—but not everything is beneficial. 'Everything is permissible'—but not everything is contructive. Nobody should seek his own good, but the good of others. . . . Do not cause anyone to stumble, whether Jews, Greeks or the church of God—even as I try to please everybody in every way. For I am not seeking my own good but the good of many, so that they may be saved" (1 Cor. 10:23-24, 32-33).

Paul makes it quite clear that we as leaders should try to remain above reproach. If you feel that is too big a price to pay, then you should reconsider your desire to be a leader.

Making Decisions Others Don't Want to Make

The late President Harry Truman had a sign on his desk that read, "The buck stops here." Effective leaders must adopt that attitude. If you are a leader, you must pay the price of sometimes making decisions others don't want to make. It is your job.

Like everyone else, you may not want to make the decision. You may not want to be responsible for the results. You may not really know what is best. But someone must decide—and that someone is you, the leader.

One of the worst things you can do is procrastinate in making a decision when one is needed. Procrastination will undermine your ability to lead. People will lose respect for you.

I am not suggesting that you should make snap decisions or be trigger-happy when it comes time to make decisions, but if a decision needs to be made, and it is your responsibility to make it, don't try to pass the buck. The price we all pay as leaders is that sometimes we have to make the decision and live with the results—whether we like it or not!

Saying No

As I mentioned earlier, effective leaders must work at keeping their emotions under control. That means that sometimes you'd really like to say yes to a request or idea, but you have to say no. There have been many times as a husband, father, and group leader that I have wanted to say yes to something, but I knew I had to say no. This can be one of the most painfully high prices we pay as leaders.

For example, my son used to be a very poor money manager. He bought anything he wanted. He would buy two or three new pairs of skis a year, just to try to keep up with the latest styles. One year I bought a new pickup truck, so my son went to town and bought a new pickup truck. I tried to tell him that he should be more responsible with his money, but it didn't seem to do any good.

One day the bank called me and explained that my son was several payments behind on his truck loan and that if he didn't get caught up, they would be forced to repossess the vehicle.

My son asked if he could borrow the money from me so he wouldn't lose his truck. I wanted to help him and say yes, but I knew he would never learn to be responsible with his money if people helped him out every time he got in a financial jam. When I told him no, I could tell he was really hurt; he felt I was letting him down, which made me feel even more like a heel.

I explained why I wasn't willing to lend him the money and suggested he go to the bank and try to work something out with them before they took his pickup. I felt so bad! I felt I was letting my son down, I felt guilty because he was so young, and I really wanted to help him avoid losing his truck. In spite of all that, I forced myself to stick by my *no* answer, even though I wanted to say yes.

It was the best thing I could have done to help my son learn to be financially responsible. He talked to the bank, got a second job, and started working to get caught up on his bills. Today my son is learning how to take care of his money, but if I had said yes to his request for help as I wanted to, he would have thought, *I don't have to worry about my debts—old Dad will always bail me out!*

The best thing was to say no, even though at the time I

really wanted to say yes. If you are a leader, you will have to learn to say no many times when your emotions tell you to say yes.

Sacrificing Personal Interests

Leaders' lives are not their own. As a leader you have a great responsibility to those you lead. You will discover that you will frequently have to be willing to sacrifice your own personal interests for the sake of the group.

Because leaders are in the people business, the needs of people should be your main concern. There have been many evenings when the phone would ring, and I would have to stop what I was doing to go meet with someone to whom I was trying to be an example.

There have been times when I hated to hear the phone ring because I knew it was someone needing to see me. No—I didn't always want to go. Yes—sometimes I resented having people intrude into what I considered to be my personal time.

However, if you are going to be an effective leader, one of the costs is the willingness to sometimes sacrifice personal interests for the good of the group.

Striving for the Best

Let's review the definition of a leader. A leader is one who leads, or guides, by showing others the way. A leader is out front offering guidance and direction and setting the pace.

You can't be a leader if you are always trying to catch up with your followers. Therefore, you must never be content with the average. You must always strive for the best—both in yourself and in those you lead.

Jesus Christ focused on setting a good example for His followers. Notice what people said about Him: "He has done everything well" (Mark 7:37). The verse also points out that because of His high performance standards, "People were overwhelmed with amazement." Paul echoes the same principle when he says, "Whatever you do, work at it with all your heart" (Col. 3:23).

IF YOU AREN'T WILLING TO PAY THE PRICE TO BECOME AN EFFECTIVE LEADER, THEN DON'T COMPLAIN ABOUT THE SHORTAGE OF LEADERS.

The Bible makes it clear that we are to give life our very best effort, and this is especially true for the leader. You can't be an average performer and expect your followers to be great performers. Followers follow the example of the leader whether the leader wants them to or not. If you want to know how your performance is, look at how much effort your followers are putting out. As a leader you set the pace!

Value People over Possessions

We have already mentioned that leaders are in the people business—people must be more important to you than material possessions.

People and possessions can't both be top priority; you have to choose one or the other. "For where your treasure is, there your heart will be also" (Matt. 6:21). If your possessions are your treasure, or top priority, then that is where your heart will be. That is where your commitment will be. You can't be an effective leader of people unless people are your priority.

If possessions are your top priority, then possessions will be the top priority of those you lead, because people *do* follow their leader. You will have a hard time getting your followers to become leaders of other people if your top priority is possessions.

If your top priority is possessions, then your followers will seek possessions first, not leading people first. Therefore, if as a leader your goal is to help your followers become leaders of people, your followers must be your top priority. They must be more important to you than possessions.

Your followers will realize the value you place in them. They will learn that the key to achieving a goal is through people, not the acquiring of possessions. And when they become leaders, they will pass on what they learned from you, and like you, they will make leaders out of their followers.

The problem with the Christian community today is that we as leaders are still trying to decide which is more important—possessions or people. And by the looks of some of our facilities, I'm afraid some of us have decided in favor of possessions.

Keeping Your Life in Balance

By now it should be apparent that it is quite easy for the leader's life to get out of balance. In fact, one of the major problems leaders have is maintaining balance in their lives. Leaders have to work harder at maintaining balanced lives than other people.

It is a price you can't afford not to pay. You must discipline yourself to focus on balance in your life. It is easy to get so caught up with leading that you expend all your energy and time leading people, leaving no time for yourself or your family. That is one of the reasons we are seeing more and more divorced Christian leaders. They tend to get so involved in the leadership functions of their ministry or business that their personal and home lives suffer. You must learn to play as hard as you work. You must learn to relax and enjoy life outside of your leadership role.

Remember, as a leader you are the example others follow whether you like it or not. If your life is out of balance, the lives of those you lead will get out of balance. Others follow what you *are*, not what you *say*.

Chapter Summary

If you want to become an effective leader, you must be willing to pay the price. No matter what you may have accomplished as a leader in the secular world, you will still need to humble yourself and invest the time and energy required to become a spiritual leader in God's business.

Even though the price of leadership is high, the rewards far outweigh the cost!

Personal Application

1. Review the costs of becoming an effective leader. If you are not a leader, but would like to be, are you willing to pay the price?
2. If you are already a leader, are you having more difficulty paying the price in some areas than in others? If so, which areas are toughest for you?
3. What could you be doing to become more committed and effective in your areas of weakness?

CHAPTER FOUR

The Formula for Revolutionizing Leadership

The term *leader* is one of the most overused and least understood words in the English language. During a recent management seminar with a group of pastors, I asked them to write sentences using the word *leader* or *lead*. Then I had them read their sentences and explain the meaning of the word *leader* in the sentence. Here are a few of the sentences and the explanations.

"He is an outstanding leader in our community" means he is very involved in community projects and highly respected and well known by people in the city.

"She is one of our leading Sunday School teachers" means she is one of our best teachers.

"We need more leaders in the church" means we need more good workers in the church.

"We have the leading church in our denomination" means we have the largest and fastest-growing church in our denomination.

"I asked Bill to lead in prayer before we started the meeting" means I asked Bill to be the one to pray before the meeting.

As you can see by the sentences and explanations, people use the words *lead* and *leader* in a wide variety of ways. In fact, we use the word *leader* so frequently and in so many different ways that many of us have lost sight of its true meaning.

When we use the word *leader,* we seldom actually mean a person who is training his followers to do what he does. Today we use the word more to show our respect and admiration for a person's accomplishments than to identify one who is guiding others along the way and training them to be future leaders.

That is one of the reasons for the leadership shortage within the Christian community today. When a leader becomes simply someone we respect and admire, we truly have lost sight of what a New Testament leader is to be.

Once the meaning of the word *leader* gets distorted, very quickly the leader's role becomes distorted also. Our watered-down version of leadership has caused us to settle for far less from our leaders than the leadership example set by Jesus Christ.

The Need for Renewal

Recently I saw a large sign in front of a church that read, "Revival services every night this week. Everyone welcome." As I drove on down the street I thought, *We don't need revival in the church; we need renewal.* For all too long we have been trying to *revive* the church instead of trying to bring about desperately needed *renewal.* And there is as much difference between revival and renewal as there is between daylight and dark.

When we focus on revival we are trying to bring a movement, organization, or person back to life. However, when an organization or person is fully revived, that group or person is no different from before the dying process began. All that has been restored is life; what caused the death is still present. Before long the sickness has gained another foothold and there is need for revival again.

It is possible to bring about revival without having renewal. Let's say the electrical system in my automobile is worn out; the wiring has lots of bare wires showing, and the battery has shorted out. I can *revive* the battery by having it recharged, and the car will start again, but the electrical shorts in the wiring will quickly cause the battery to run down again and I'll have to get the battery recharged again. Recharging the battery *revives* it, but it doesn't eliminate the problem that caused it to go dead in the first place.

IT ISN'T WHAT YOU DO BUT WHAT YOU TEACH OTHERS TO DO THAT MAKES YOU A GREAT LEADER.

To solve my car's starting problem I need *renewal*. I need to replace the old, worn-out wiring with new wiring. I need to install a new battery in place of the old one.

This crude example helps illustrate the need for leadership renewal in the Christian community. Instead of continually trying to revive the old, ineffective, traditional approach to leadership, we need a renewal of New Testament principles of leadership.

Renewal isn't just innovation and change. It is the restoration of the original state of existence. Within Christendom we desperately need to restore the type of leadership practiced originally by Jesus Christ and the early church.

If you want to become an effective leader, study the life and actions of Jesus Christ. He is the greatest leader the world has ever seen. No other leader in history accomplished so much in such a short period of time or had as great an impact on the entire world as Jesus Christ. Once they examine His life, even people who don't accept Him as their personal Lord and Saviour have to admit He was a very successful leader.

A close evaluation of Jesus Christ's life reveals that He took a revolutionary approach to leadership. He departed from many of the traditions of His day as He personally applied and trained His followers in what I have come to call New Testament principles of leadership.

_____

IT ISN'T HOW WELL YOU START BUT HOW YOU FINISH THAT COUNTS.

_____

We must keep in mind that it isn't what you do but what you teach others to do that makes you a great leader. That is why Jesus was the greatest leader the world has ever seen. Teaching His followers to do what He did was His top priority as a leader.

Jesus Christ's Purpose as a Leader

The prayer of Jesus that is recorded in the seventeenth chapter of John is one of the most important prayers recorded in the Bible. It gives us a close-up view of Jesus Christ's approach to leadership. Every Christian leader should do a verse-by-verse study of this prayer.

Notice what Jesus tells God the Father in John 17:4. "I have brought You glory on earth by completing the work You gave Me to do." This prayer was prayed prior to Jesus' death on the cross, so He couldn't have been referring to His death for the remission of our sins. But what had He accomplished that motivated Him to make that statement? He gives us the answer in verses 6-23.

In verse 6 Jesus said, "I have revealed You to those whom You gave Me out of the world." In verse 8 He continued, "For I gave them the words You gave Me and they accepted them." In verse 12 we read, "While I was with them, I protected them and kept them safe," and in verse 18, "As You sent Me into the world, I have sent them into the world." John 17 is not only a prayer from Jesus to the Father. It is a description of how Jesus worked as a leader. Verse 18 gives us a clear picture of Jesus Christ's purpose in leading His disciples, to make leaders out of them.

When Jesus told His Father He had completed His work, He had not healed every sick person in the world. He had not cast out all of the demons. He had not fed all of the starving and hungry people. He hadn't even gone to the cross yet. But He had completed the task of training His disciples to do what He did.

Jesus Christ's stated goal was to help His followers learn to do what He did (John 14:12). Luke records a picture of Jesus training His twelve disciples to do what He was doing. He gave them the responsibility and power to cast out demons and heal the sick. He also taught them to go out and preach the Good News to the lost and dying world (Luke 9:1-6).

Jesus focused on "performance reproduction"—He reproduced Himself and His performance in the lives of His followers. He spent three years training twelve followers to do what He did. He not only traveled around the countryside preaching the Gospel and healing the sick, He trained His followers to do the same and sent them out with the same mission.

Notice His instructions to the twelve disciples in Matthew 10:5-8: "These twelve Jesus sent out with the following instructions: . . . 'As you go, preach this message: "The kingdom of heaven is near." Heal the sick, raise the dead, cleanse those who have leprosy, drive out demons. Freely you have received, freely give.' "

That is exactly what Jesus Christ had been doing. He had been preaching the message that the kingdom of heaven was near. He had been healing the sick, raising the dead, cleansing those with leprosy, driving out demons, and freely giving of Himself to those in need. He didn't see His function as a leader as simply gathering followers while He performed His tasks. His job was to train His followers to do exactly what He did. And the completion of that job brought glory to God (John 17:4).

Commanded to Lead as Jesus Led

Jesus Christ's job wasn't just to train His followers to be leaders. He commanded them to do what He did—make leaders out of their followers.

Matthew 28:18-20 gives us the great command to go make leaders out of our followers and teach them to do what we are doing. "Then Jesus came to them and said . . . 'Go and make disciples of all nations . . . teaching them to obey everything I have commanded you.'"

Once Jesus had trained His followers to become leaders like Himself, He commanded them to go make disciples (or followers) in every nation in the world and teach those followers to obey everything Jesus had taught them—which included making disciples. The Great Commission is more than a command to reach the world with the Gospel. It also provides the plan for accomplishing that end.

Jesus knew that any movement had to have effective leaders in order to grow and spread to the entire world. Therefore, this Great Commission was actually a commission to carry on the mission that Jesus Christ started. This is how a movement begins and like a tidal wave spreads across the entire world.

THE QUESTION ISN'T "HOW MANY FOLLOWERS DO YOU HAVE?" IT'S "HOW MANY LEADERS ARE YOU DEVELOPING?"

Paul wrote Timothy a formula for making disciples of Jesus Christ, which is also a revolutionary formula for developing effective leaders who in turn know how to develop effective leaders. "And the things you have heard me say in the presence of many witnesses entrust to reliable men who will also be qualified to teach others" (2 Tim. 2:2). This verse has become one of the foundation verses for the call to make disciples for Jesus Christ. It also teaches the very heart of New Testament leadership principles. It commands us to turn followers into leaders who will turn followers into leaders.

Leaders in the Christian community must be willing to break with the traditional approach to leadership and become one of the "new leaders" committed to applying the leadership principles taught by Jesus Christ. There is no greater leadership challenge than the challenge to help our followers become leaders capable of training their followers to be leaders also.

A Leader's Purpose

One of the things that made Jesus Christ a great leader is His ability to never lose sight of His real purpose as a leader. From the time He called His first disciples saying, "Come, follow Me...and I will make you fishers of men" (Matt. 4:19), Jesus always focused on training His followers to be effective leaders like Himself.

My college basketball coach used to say, "Always keep in mind that it isn't how well you start the game but how you finish that counts!" I recently watched the Kentucky Derby, and the horse that won the race was in last place when the race began. Many leaders start strong but finish poorly. They have great ability to recruit followers and set the pace as their example, but they never seem to be able to turn their followers into leaders like themselves. One of the reasons this occurs is that it is easy to lose sight of the real goal of leadership. Leaders are busy people, and the busier they are the easier it is to lose sight of the real purpose of leadership.

Many would-be leaders wind up becoming performers because they get caught in the activity trap. They find themselves spending all of their time working for their followers instead of training their followers to do for themselves.

As a result, the would-be leader slowly loses sight of the real purpose of training followers to be leaders and begins to focus on performing for the followers. As long as that continues, the would-be leader will never be able to apply the principles of leadership practiced by Jesus.

Jesus Christ always made sure people didn't get Him so busy He didn't have time to properly train His followers (Mark 6:30-32). No matter how busy His schedule, Jesus never lost sight of the need to spend time training His followers to become leaders.

You may be an excellent recruiter of people. You may be able to set the pace and point the way for others to follow. But how many of your followers are becoming leaders like yourself? The question isn't "How many followers do you have?" It's "How many leaders are you developing?"

Every good leader has two purposes. One is the purpose or cause he is giving his life to. This first purpose is the one that motivates him to step forward and volunteer to set an example for others to follow. Once he has people following him who have the same purpose in life as he does, the good leader develops a second purpose.

The second purpose is to train the followers to be effective leaders so that the first purpose can be accomplished more quickly and effectively.

Most traditional leaders clearly understand the first purpose, but in order to apply New Testament principles of leadership we must develop the second purpose as well.

What Is Your Purpose?

Do you want to be an effective leader? Then you must first develop a meaningful personal purpose for your life. A leader without a purpose is like a ship without a compass.

Purpose is what motivates you to action. Your purpose is the vehicle that moves you and others to make a commitment. Purpose moves people from the seat to their feet. It is the single most important ingredient for recruiting followers and making them willing to become leaders.

People who are headed nowhere get there every time. It is

impossible to be an effective leader without first developing a clearly defined purpose. What is your purpose? Answering that question is the first step in becoming a strong leader.

Your purpose must be put in writing and reviewed regularly by yourself and your followers. It is very important for the leader to develop a purpose statement and put it in writing. Writing it down forces you to think it through carefully. It also helps plant it firmly in your mind.

Once you have your purpose statement in writing, put it in a place where you can review it regularly. There is no value in developing a written purpose statement unless you are willing to review it on a regular basis.

By having your purpose statement in writing, you are also better prepared to share it with others. You will be able to be consistent in presenting it, which is very important.

Once when I was conducting a long-range planning workshop for staff and board members of a large church, I asked each person to write down what they considered to be the purpose of the church. To their surprise, there were many differences of opinion among both staff and board members.

Some thought the church's purpose was to train the people to "do the work of the ministry," and they quoted Ephesians 4:11-12 to support their belief. Others saw the church as the place where non-Christians should be brought to hear the Gospel so they could be challenged to accept Jesus Christ. A few thought that the church's purpose was to promote brotherly love and demonstrate that love by meeting the needs of the hurting people in the community.

As the group began sharing with one another what they had written, the pastor said, "I can see why we have had such a problem agreeing among ourselves during our business meetings. We all have different views of our purpose as a church."

We spent the next few hours developing a mutually acceptable written purpose. At the conclusion of that exercise one of the board members said, "This is the first time I've felt like we all understand where we are headed as a church—

and that really excites me!"

During lunch the senior pastor said, "I guess I just assumed we all understood the purpose of the church." He and I rode together from the restaurant back to the church where we were conducting the workshop. As we drove into the church parking lot, he said, "For a long time I've felt we lacked strong unity within our group. I think we solved that problem this morning when we took the time to develop a written purpose."

As he parked the car he put his hand on my shoulder and exclaimed, "Isn't it amazing how we as leaders can get so busy with all of the activity that we overlook something so important as making sure we all understand the purpose?"

Yes, it is amazing! But most of us have been guilty of it from time to time. If you want to be an effective leader you must develop a written purpose statement. That statement must be clearly understood by all of your followers.

Be Selective

In order to be an effective leader, you must have committed followers. Most leaders are very committed to their purpose, otherwise they would not have taken it upon themselves to step forward and set the example for others to follow. However, it isn't enough for leaders to be committed to their purpose. They must also have followers committed to their purpose and willing to follow their example as well.

You cannot have committed leaders until you first have committed followers. The lack of strong commitment to the cause of Jesus Christ is one of the reasons we have such a shortage of leaders within Christendom today. The local church has lost its ability to require commitment from its followers. As a matter of fact, it is the only organization I know where you aren't required to do anything in order to join, you aren't required to do anything once you are a member, and you aren't required to do anything in order to remain a member.

Modern Christianity has chosen to sacrifice commitment in order to have *quantity* instead of *quality*. We are rapidly moving toward a philosophy that places greater emphasis on the size of the crowd than on the depth of its commitment.

Jesus Christ operated much differently as a leader. He placed far greater emphasis on quality than he did quantity. Even though Jesus Christ's goal was to reach the entire world with the Good News of the Gospel, He knew that *commitment* always precedes *conquest*. He realized that the height of one's achievement is in direct proportion to the depth of one's commitment.

Jesus always placed high demands on His followers, because that is the way you develop commitment. The higher the demand, the greater the commitment. On the other hand, the lower the demand, the less the commitment.

THE LOCAL CHURCH IS THE ONLY ORGANIZATION I KNOW WHERE YOU AREN'T REQUIRED TO DO ANYTHING IN ORDER TO JOIN, YOU AREN'T REQUIRED TO DO ANYTHING ONCE YOU ARE A MEMBER, AND YOU AREN'T REQUIRED TO DO ANYTHING TO REMAIN A MEMBER!

Knowing this, one day Jesus turned to a large crowd of people following Him and said, "Anyone who wants to be My follower must love Me far more than he does his own father, mother, wife, children, brothers, or sisters—yes, more than his own life—otherwise he cannot be My disciple. And no one can be My disciple who does not carry his own cross and follow Me" (Luke 14:26-27, TLB).

Jesus wanted the multitudes to know that He demanded commitment from His followers. He wasn't interested in the quantity of people following Him; He wanted quality, and that required a strong commitment on the part of followers. Jesus Christ certainly didn't measure His success in terms of the size of the crowd following Him.

That doesn't seem to be true of many of our modern-day traditional leaders. For them, success is frequently measured in terms of the magnitude of the crowd and the size of the offering. But generally speaking, very little is said about the depth of the commitment.

Again, I must use Communism as a modern-day example of the type of commitment Jesus Christ demanded from His followers. Many years ago Billy Graham publicly read a now-famous letter written by a young American college student who had been attracted to Communism while in Mexico. The student was writing to his fiancee, explaining that he must break their engagement because he was now totally committed to the Communist cause. Here is part of that letter:

> We Communists have a high casualty rate. We're the ones who get shot and hung and lynched and tarred and feathered and jailed and slandered, and ridiculed and fired from our jobs, and in every other way made as uncomfortable as possible. A certain percentage of us get killed or imprisoned. We live in virtual poverty. We turn back to the party every penny we make above what is absolutely necessary to keep us alive. We Communists don't have the time or the money for many movies, or concerts, or T-bone steaks, or decent homes and new cars. We've been described as fanatics. We are fanatics. Our lives are dominated by one great overshadowing factor, THE STRUGGLE FOR WORLD COMMUNISM.
>
> We Communists have a philosophy of life which no amount of money could buy. We have a cause to fight for, a definite purpose in life. We subordinate our petty, personal selves into a great movement of humanity, and if our personal lives seem hard, or our egos appear to

suffer through subordination to the party, then we are adequately compensated by the thought that each of us in his small way is contributing to something new and true and better for mankind. There is one thing in which I am in dead earnest and that is the Communist cause. It is my life, my business, my religion, my hobby, my sweetheart, my wife and mistress, my bread and meat. I work at it in the daytime and dream of it at night. Its hold on me grows, not lessens, as time goes on. Therefore, I cannot carry on a friendship, a love affair, or even a conversation without relating it to the force which both drives and guides my life. I evaluate people, books, ideas and actions according to how they affect the Communist cause and by their attitude toward it. I've already been in jail because of my ideas and if necessary, I'm ready to go before a firing squad.

Do you want to know why Communism is steadily marching around the globe? Because its leaders know how to motivate their followers to make strong commitments to the Communist cause. Anyone can believe in the communist philosophy, but only the very committed are allowed to be members of the party.

WHEN YOU REQUIRE NOTHING FROM YOUR FOLLOWERS, YOU GET NOTHING IN RETURN.

The same is true with Christianity. Anyone can believe in Jesus Christ, but He did not allow everyone to become one of His inner circle of followers, the Twelve. He was selective concerning whom He trained to be leaders.

For example, Jesus once cast demons out of a man who in turn asked to go with Him. "Jesus did not let him, but said,

'Go home to your family and tell them how much the Lord has done for you, and how He has had mercy on you.' So the man went away and began to tell in the Decapolis how much Jesus had done for him. And all the people were amazed" (Mark 5:19-20).

This man obviously believed in Jesus and wanted to become one of His disciples. However, Jesus did not take all volunteers to join the Twelve. He was very selective. And that is the mark of an effective leader.

If your goal is to perform for an audience, then the more people following you the merrier. However, if your goal is to be an effective leader and train your followers to do what you do as Jesus did, then you must limit the number of people you allow to follow you.

Before I go further with this discussion I want to make it very clear that I am not suggesting that we should bar people from attending or joining a church. Christ died for everyone. And it is my desire that every person come to know Jesus Christ as personal Lord and Saviour.

However, we are talking about principles of New Testament leadership. And even though Jesus preached to the masses and wanted everyone to believe in Him, He was very selective concerning who became part of His inner circle of disciples.

Jesus invited many people to follow Him who turned down the offer because the commitment requirements were too high for them. He never lowered His standards in order to draw more people to follow Him.

Unfortunately, that isn't always the case with leaders in modern Christianity. When we measure our success in terms of the number of followers we have, we are frequently tempted to lower the requirements and demands to enable more people to follow us.

The lower the requirements for followers, the lower the commitment of followers. The lower the commitment of the followers, the fewer people there will be to step forward and volunteer to be leaders for others to follow.

That is why we frequently find churches with many people, but not enough volunteers to teach Sunday School or work in the nursery. When you require nothing from your followers, you get nothing in return.

Chapter Summary
For all practical purposes we have lost the meaning of the word *leader* as demonstrated by Jesus Christ and the early church. When a leader is nothing more than someone we respect and admire for his personal accomplishments, we have truly lost sight of the New Testament idea of leadership. Our modern, watered-down version of the meaning of leadership has caused us to settle for far less from our leaders than the leadership example set by Jesus Christ.

Personal Application
1. Ask a group of your peers to write a sentence using the word *lead* or *leader*. Then ask them to read the sentence and explain what they meant by *lead* or *leader*. How do their definitions fit the idea of a leader as portrayed by Jesus Christ?
2. Study Jesus Christ's prayer in John 17 and list the leadership principles you see Him describing.
3. Study Matthew 28:18-20 and 2 Timothy 2:2. As a leader, do you feel you are currently applying the leadership principles taught in these passages? If not, what will you do to begin applying them?
4. What is your personal purpose in life? If you have never done so before, make a written statement of your life purpose.
5. If you are a leader, meet with your followers and have each person write out what they feel the group's purpose is. Have each person report. If there are differences of opinion concerning what the purpose should be, have the group develop a purpose together.

6. As a leader, have you been focusing on quality or quantity?
7. Develop a specific set of requirements for people to meet in order to be one of your followers.

CHAPTER FIVE

Developing Unity
in the Midst of Discord

There has never been a time in world history when the need for unity among Christians was as great as it is today. While the church faces increasing criticism and attacks from without, it is being steadily undermined and weakened from within.

The great societies of the world are currently riding the high crests of the tidal waves of major ideological change. Longstanding traditional values and beliefs are rapidly being abandoned all over the world as multitudes in all walks of life and from every corner of the earth are falling in step with the movement to usher in the so-called New Age of enlightenment dawning on the near horizon.

Leaders in the New Age movement are quietly but quickly bringing about major social, educational, political, and religious reforms that are already greatly affecting every area of our lives. They are well along in their plans to usher in a world government in the near future.

The ideology of the New Age movement (which teaches that the road to spiritual enlightenment is through contact with one's "higher self") is emerging as one of the greatest threats to the modern church. And yet many Christians are so busy fighting among themselves that they have little if any energy left to withstand this attack of the enemy at their doorstep.

The Real Enemy

As surprising as it may be to some Christians, the evil forces attacking the church from without are not the *real* enemy of Christianity. The Bible clearly states that as long as God lives in us, Satan is powerless in his attempt to destroy us (1 John 4:4; James 4:7). If the forces of Satan were able to overpower the church, it would have been destroyed long ago. However, notice Jesus' statement in Matthew 16:18: "On this rock I will build My church, and the gates of Hades will not overcome it." This verse assures us that Satan will never be able to destroy God's church.

There remains an enemy capable of destroying the church, and this enemy is rapidly rendering Christendom powerless. The church will never be destroyed from without, but it is well on its way to being annihilated from within.

The church's *real* enemy is the dissension, discord, infighting, and lack of unity in its own ranks. Unless God's people start pulling together, God's church will soon be pulled apart. We must realize we will never win the fight against the forces of Satan as long as we are so busy fighting among ourselves. The church has become its own worst enemy.

Notice Paul's statement to the church at Galatia: "If you keep on biting and devouring each other, watch out or you will be destroyed by each other" (Gal. 5:15). Paul was warning the people that their church was on the verge of being destroyed from within because of their lack of unity. The same type of disunity Paul observed in the church almost two thousand years ago is even greater today.

While Catholics fight Protestants, Protestants are busy destroying one another. Each group tends to set itself up as the authority by which all others should be judged. This feeling of superior spirituality is one of the main reasons for disunity and decay in the organized church today.

This superior spirituality syndrome has plagued the church from antiquity. In 2 Corinthians 10 Paul deals with this issue. He writes, "We do not dare to classify or compare ourselves with some who commend themselves. When they measure themselves and compare themselves with themselves, they are not wise. . . . But, 'Let him who boasts boast in the Lord.' For it is not the man who commends himself who is approved, but the man whom the Lord commends" (vv. 12, 17-18).

**UNLESS GOD'S PEOPLE
START PULLING TOGETHER,
GOD'S CHURCH WILL SOON
BE PULLED APART.**

Paul's words are just as needed and relevant today as they were when he wrote them to the church at Corinth. The people were using their own level of spiritual convictions, growth, and maturity as the measuring stick by which all others were judged. But it isn't our own self-righteousness that makes us righteous, but God's approval alone.

The modern institutional church desperately needs to learn what Paul is teaching us in 2 Corinthians 10. God never intended for the church to be a "spiritual police state" with a religious caste system. He expects and requires that His people love one another in harmony and unity. Notice the instructions Jesus Christ gave us in John 13:34-35. "And so I am giving a new commandment to you now—love each other just as much as I love you. Your strong love for each other will prove to the world that you are My disciples" (TLB).

God intended the church's trademark to be strong love for one another. How does the world see Christians today? As people who fight among themselves, who can't get along with each other, who quarrel over even the most minor points in their religious beliefs, who criticize rather than support one another, and who display great intolerance for other Christians who disagree with their personal religious beliefs.

It isn't the power of Satan's forces, it's the discord in the organized church that is rendering it powerless and helpless in combating the forces of evil.

Unity Starts with Leadership

As a management consultant I have the opportunity to work with a wide variety of religious organizations across this country and around the world. I have worked with religious leaders from many denominations and theological persuasions. I have observed that as a general rule leaders of Christian groups are reluctant to cooperate wholeheartedly with other Christian groups. Often, even leaders of churches of the same denomination and in the same community are unwilling to cooperate with one another.

I recently held a public seminar on burnout in Colorado. I usually hold public seminars in hotels or convention centers, but a friend of mine, the senior pastor of a large church in the community, invited me to use the church's fine facilities as a meeting place.

I accepted his offer but quickly discovered I had made a big mistake. Because my friend's church was a mainline denomination's largest church in the community, I assumed that the other churches associated with that denomination in the area would readily cooperate in promoting the seminar. I soon learned I was wrong.

Once the brochures for the seminar were printed, I set appointments with the other pastors representing churches within that denomination and began promoting the seminar. The pastor of the denomination's second largest church in the city quickly let me know he would not promote the seminar in his church. He wouldn't even take a brochure. He said, "The only reason they are hosting the seminar is to try to attract people from our smaller churches to come and visit their great facilities and then maybe they will start attending there instead of the smaller church."

He was very angry as he continued. "They have built their church by stealing members from our smaller churches! And one of the ways they do it is by sponsoring these kinds of programs. I'll have no part of it, and I won't even let my people know it's being held there!"

The next day I met with the senior pastor of another denomination's church in the city. When I asked if he would be interested in some brochures and whether he would announce the seminar in the church's bulletin he replied, "We only promote programs sponsored by our own denomination."

I left the pastor's study feeling frustrated and angry, not because he wasn't willing to promote a seminar I was conducting, but because of the lack of cooperation I saw among the Christian leaders in the city. They had not learned the wisdom of the saying, "When two hands wash each other, they both get clean."

As I walked to my car, I was reminded of the time I first met Dr. Milton Cook, a medical doctor who, along with his entire family, had accepted Jesus Christ at a Billy Graham Crusade and then started attending church. Dr. Cook and his wife, Doris, were very excited about their new-found faith and eagerly accepted the invitation to get involved in a small-group Bible study.

A few weeks after the Graham crusade was over, Milton and Doris met me in a parking lot one morning and with big smiles showed me a large poster promoting a Gospel singing group scheduled to hold a weekend crusade in the city auditorium.

A quick glance at the religious terminology used to promote the services told me that this group held a different view of the gifts of the Spirit than what is taught by the church the Cooks were attending. Milton said, "I'm going to ask our pastor to post this on the bulletin board. I'm sure there will be a lot of people from the church interested in attending."

WHEN TWO HANDS WASH EACH OTHER, THEY BOTH GET CLEAN.

That afternoon Doris called my home in tears. "You've got to come over right away," she said. "Milton threw our Bible in the garbage can and swears he will never go to church again!" She was so upset I couldn't understand what she was trying to tell me over the phone, so I told her I would be right over.

When I arrived at the Cooks' home I found two very hurt and angry people. After leaving me that morning, they had approached one of the associate pastors of their church and requested permission to post the flyer promoting the singing group's crusade on the church bulletin board.

The pastor had not only refused to let them put the poster on the church bulletin board, but had also lectured them concerning the "errors" of the group's theological beliefs. "He told us groups like this just play on people's emotions and he said something about them really not understanding the right way to be Christians," Doris said. "He acted like they were bad people or something and we shouldn't have anything to do with people who believe like that."

I spent the rest of the afternoon listening to Milton and Doris vent their frustrations. They had accepted Jesus Christ at a religious crusade and they were excited about the opportunity to have other people attend this one to hear about Jesus Christ and the difference He could make in people's lives. However, a few short weeks after becoming Christians they had been exposed to the type of conflicts and open hostilities that frequently occur among the various groups within God's family. They very quickly became disillusioned with the church.

Milton and Doris are still my friends, but they don't attend church anymore. Occasionally we get together over coffee or lunch and discuss our religious convictions. Milton and Doris recently returned from India where they had been studying under one of the Hindu "enlightened ones." Both Milton and Doris put on workshops around the country to teach people how to meditate in order to "contact the god within you." They are very critical of Christianity and are quick to tell their own experience with a church as "proof" that Christians don't know the true meaning of love and how to practice it.

As I got in my car that day after being told by the pastor of an evangelical church, "We only promote programs sponsored by our own denomination," I lay my head on the steering wheel of my car and cried. I wondered how many other people like Milton and Doris we have driven away because of our disunity.

The need for unity is greater today than ever before in the history of the church. It is time the rest of the world recognizes us as being part of God's family because of our deep love for one another. It is time for our leaders to recognize that unity begins with leadership.

As we have already pointed out, followers do follow the leader whether he or she sets a good example or not. In order to have harmony and unity in an organization, there must first be harmony and unity among its leaders.

The church does not need more leaders with more academic degrees after their names. The church desperately needs more leaders with a renewed commitment to love. We are living in a time when our leaders must learn to stand together, or our churches will soon fall completely apart.

A popular Christian song goes, "We are one in the Spirit, we are one in the Lord." Demonstrating that oneness should be the goal of every Christian leader in every church and

Christian organization.

The Cause of Disunity

There are many factors that contribute to disunity in the church today. However, it should be noted that disunity is a *symptom* of a problem—it is not the problem itself—and in order to be effective leaders we must learn to deal with the cause and not just the effect. Disunity is the effect, not the cause.

Unity is love in action; disunity is the absence of love in action. The lack of unity in the church is the result of the lack of love within God's people. In many instances not only do we fail to love a lost and dying world, we don't even like our brothers and sisters in God's family.

The effective leader combats disunity by concentrating on teaching followers the necessity of developing strong bonds of love between one another. The need for love was one of the central themes of Jesus Christ's messages to the world and especially to His inner circle of disciples. "My command is this: Love each other as I have loved you" (John 15:12).

Jesus *commanded* His followers to love one another—it wasn't an option. That is one of the things that made Jesus a great leader—He knew the great importance of developing a group of followers who had strong love for one another. Therefore, the leaders who want to follow New Testament principles of leadership must focus on the importance of loving one another. Like Jesus, they must make love for one another one of the *requirements* for followers. If Jesus Christ made brotherly love a requirement, how dare we do any less!

One of the main reasons there is so much discord in Christendom today is that our Christian leaders do not follow Jesus Christ's example to demonstrate love and make brotherly love a requirement in the group of followers. Jesus was the role model for His followers. Jesus Christ loved people so much He gave His life for them.

The Results of Love

Love is not just an attitude; it is an action. There is no value in my saying "I love you" unless my actions back up my words. Christians today do a lot of talking about love, but in many instances our actions don't back up what we say—our *walk* doesn't support our *talk*. "If anyone has material possessions and sees his brother in need but has no pity on him, how can the love of God be in him? Dear children, let us not love with words or tongue but with actions and in truth" (1 John 3:17-18).

Love produces positive actions, and the environment created by those positive actions is what we call unity. On the other hand, the absence of love produces negative actions, and the environment created is what we call disunity or discord. Therefore, the effective leader focuses on modeling and requiring brotherly love among followers.

Consider love as described in 1 Corinthians 13:4-8.

Love is patient, love is kind. It does not envy, it does not boast, it is not proud. It is not rude, it is not self-seeking, it is not easily angered, it keeps no record of wrongs. Love does not delight in evil but rejoices with the truth. It always protects, always trusts, always hopes, always perseveres. Love never fails.

By studying the actions of love in this passage, we can see why Jesus Christ placed such strong emphasis on love and made it a requirement for His disciples. In every instance love produces a positive result.

Later in the book we will devote an entire chapter to the subject of how to incorporate these actions into an effective leadership style.

First Step

Since unity is the result of brotherly love in action, the starting point for developing unity in a group is to decide to adopt 1 Corinthians 13:4-8 as a lifestyle in the group. Since the actions described in these verses are not always compatible with our selfish human nature, we must make conscious decisions to act and react in love. Just as Jesus Christ commanded His followers to love one another, so effective leaders today must command their followers to love one another.

If Christians obeyed Jesus Christ's command to love one another, the world would be beating the doors of our churches down trying to get in, because every person wants to be treated the way 1 Corinthians 13:4-8 tells us to treat them. If you are the leader of a group applying the principles described in this passage you won't ever need to worry about where you will find people to join your group—people will be begging you to let them join.

However, you can't expect your followers to apply the principles in this passage unless you, their leader, set the example. Let's look again at the definition of the new leader as stated in the first chapter. The new leader recruits people to follow his example and guides them along the way while he is teaching them to do what he does. Leaders must recognize that they reproduce what they *do* and not just what they *say* or recommend.

Christian followers are simply following their leaders. When the leaders of our Christian organizations and churches don't love one another, we certainly can't expect their followers to. However, as our leaders begin to apply the principles of leadership taught by Jesus Christ and set the example for their groups to follow, we will see one of the greatest spiritual awakenings the world has ever seen.

Chapter Summary

Unity is one of the greatest needs facing the Christian church. The church is pressured and threatened by the forces of Satan on every front. Many people are saying the days of the church are numbered. Yet many Christians are so busy fighting among themselves they can't withstand the enemy's attacks. The starting point for developing unity is to have all of us adopt 1 Corinthians 13:4-8 as the way of relating to others.

Personal Application

1. What factors cause disunity in the church?
2. What steps could Christian leaders take to create better unity among God's people?
3. Read John 13:34-35 and John 15:12 and make a list of actions you plan to take to more effectively implement these passages.
4. Develop a personal action plan concerning the part you intend to play in creating stronger unity in your home, in your church, among your followers, and in the Christian community where you live.

CHAPTER SIX

An Effective Leader Is an Effective Servant

In the secular world, leadership takes on many different faces and styles. A multitude of books have been written and speeches given to explain and define the various methods used and roles played by leaders. Historians meticulously study the events of world history and the people who shaped them and attempt to explain to us what made these leaders great.

For the past several decades psychologists, sociologists, philosophers, educators, and management consultants have been spending enormous quantities of time, money, and energy to discover and explain to the rest of the waiting world the magic formula for producing effective leaders. In recent years almost every university, college, and business school has jumped on the leadership bandwagon by offering courses, seminars, and workshops on the techniques of effective leadership. All the while, as one leadership theory after another is paraded by, our institutions keep informing us of the growing shortage of competent leaders.

You can relax, because I will not bore you by attempting to explain all these leadership theories in this chapter. There are plenty of books already in print on the subject and you will find they make good substitutes for sleeping pills on nights you have trouble sleeping.

Since this book focuses on biblical principles of leadership, primarily those taught and practiced by the world's most effective leader, Jesus Christ, we will spend our time in this chapter looking at the type of leadership style He used and make that our role model. We will also compare Jesus Christ's leadership style and philosophy with that of the secular world and evaluate the results of both.

The Focal Point of Leadership

The focal point of leadership is power. Every leader has a certain amount of power. In secular organizational structures, the higher up the organizational ladder one climbs, the more power there is available in each position. The exact amount of power available in each leadership position is always determined by the individual leader's ability and skill to generate and hold on to power. However, it isn't how much power you have, but what you do with it that determines your greatness as a leader.

Power is neither good nor bad. What the leader chooses to do with that power determines whether it is positive or negative. Abraham Lincoln used the Union army and the power of his position as President of the United States to free the slaves in this country. Adolf Hitler used the German army and the power of his position as head of the German nation to kill millions of Jews and try to control the entire world.

Throughout human history power has been the most sought after and prized possession. People never get enough power. People eventually get tired of too much sex, fame, and all the things money can buy, but they never seem to satisfy their appetite for power.

Human history is primarily the record of our quest for power to control our own future and destiny and the future and destiny of others. Every battle in every war ever fought, no matter how small or large, has been the result of our unquenchable thirst for power and control.

Power to Serve

Jesus Christ spent three years training His twelve disciples to be the future leaders responsible for organizing the early church and launching it into a worldwide ministry. These twelve men had little, if any, formal leadership training before they joined Jesus' ministry team. One was a tax collector, and several had made their living as commercial fishermen—not exactly the kind of group you would think to pick to start and maintain a worldwide organization. These were people like you and me. They had the same needs, concerns, and motivations that we do. They worried about paying the bills just as most of us do today. And they wanted to climb the organizational ladder in search of what we call success just like any other high achiever. These twelve people were just like any other twelve people sitting in the church pews of any church in the world.

One day a situation developed in which Jesus realized the twelve disciples were in serious need of a crash course in leadership training. The event is recorded in Matthew 20. One day the mother of two of the disciples, James and John, came to Jesus with a request. "Grant that one of these two sons of mine may sit at Your right and the other at Your left in Your kingdom" (v. 21).

IT ISN'T HOW MUCH POWER YOU HAVE BUT WHAT YOU DO WITH IT THAT DETERMINES YOUR GREATNESS AS A LEADER.

Notice her request. She was asking Jesus to give her two sons the two top positions immediately under Jesus in His organization. She wanted her two sons to have the power that went with the position—and I bet her two sons put her up to making the request! Isn't that amazing? Even two thousand years ago people were already involved in the rat race of trying to climb the organizational ladder.

Jesus explains to this enterprising mother that He doesn't have the authority to select the people for those positions; His Father, the chairman of the board, makes those decisions. Notice the reaction of the other ten disciples when they discovered that James and John's mother had made that request. "When the ten heard about this, they were indignant with the two brothers" (v. 24). Why were the rest of the disciples angry? Because they all wanted the two top slots in the organization too! They were just as power hungry as James and John. Jesus recognized this and knew He had a serious problem. He called a meeting with the twelve disciples and explained the difference between the way the secular world approaches leadership and His way.

Notice Jesus' instructions to the disciples in verses 25-28.

> You know that the rulers of the Gentiles lord it over them, and their high officials exercise authority over them. Not so with you. Instead, whoever wants to become great among you must be your servant, and whoever wants to be first must be your slave—just as the Son of Man did not come to be served, but to serve, and to give His life as a ransom for many.

I can almost hear them muttering under their breath, "Have You gone mad? No one leads an organization the way You are suggesting! Everyone knows that once you work your way up the ladder you deserve the power, authority, recognition, and prestige that goes with the position!"

A LEADER WILL USE POWER ONE OF TWO WAYS: TO SERVE OR TO BE SERVED.

Let's take a closer look at what Jesus was saying. He begins by pointing out that in the secular world, power is used to enable the leader to be served by the followers and control them, but He also makes it very clear that in His organization leaders will not operate that way.

If we want to be leaders in Jesus Christ's organization, we *must* serve our followers. Notice that word *must* each time it is used in the passage. Jesus meant what He said—there are no exceptions. There are no loopholes.

In the secular world people feel leaders have a right to use the power of their position to meet their own interests and needs. The secular world says, "He paid his dues to get to the top; now he has a right to enjoy the fruit of his labor. Jesus Christ says, "Whoever wants to become great among you must be your servant, and whoever wants to be first must be your slave."

There are two options for leaders—follow the world's way or follow Jesus Christ's way. A leader will use power one of two ways: to serve or to be served. If you are a leader, you have a choice to make. Which philosophy of leadership will you follow—the secular world's or Jesus Christ's?

Why Are We So Reluctant to Serve?

At an ever-increasing rate, Christians are replacing biblical truths with secular theories and principles. That certainly is the case in the field of leadership and organizational dynamics. For the most part, Christians have bought the world's philosophies of leadership hook, line, and sinker. Why? The answer is simple. Like people in the secular world we don't want to give up the power that goes with the position. It is often just as difficult for the Christian leader to assume the role of a servant as for the non-Christian.

It may have been easier for the twelve disciples to follow Jesus' leadership example because He was their mentor on a daily basis and served as a living example of a servant leader in action. Today, however, not many Christians have had a mentor who was a servant leader. Most Christian leaders have been trained in secular leadership, so we have a shortage of active, living, servant-leader role models.

The servant-leader principle taught and practiced by Jesus Christ had a profound influence on His followers and was one of the reasons for the rapid growth of the early church. Many of the writers of the New Testament opened their letters by identifying themselves as servants.

Another reason Christendom is reluctant to follow Jesus Christ's example of leadership is that more and more people are no longer convinced the principles taught in the Bible are relevant to our modern world. We are fast approaching a time in Christendom when the majority of our religious leaders would rather debate the Bible's validity than apply its principles.

When a football team performs poorly game after game, the coach takes the team back to the basics. Practice sessions are spent working on the fundamentals of blocking, tackling, passing, running, and so on. Today Christendom is like the football team that is losing game after game. We are no longer an effective light for a lost and hurting world. Many of our once-strong mainline denominations are rapidly losing members. Church doors are being closed as Sunday after Sunday church pulpits are left unfilled. At the same time philosophies like Communism and the New Age movement are steadily gaining ground.

WE ARE FAST APPROACHING A TIME WHEN THE MAJORITY OF OUR RELIGIOUS LEADERS WOULD RATHER DEBATE THE BIBLE'S VALIDITY THAN APPLY ITS PRINCIPLES.

Christians need to get back to basics. We need to relearn the principles taught and practiced by Jesus Christ and make

Him our leadership mentor. Only then will the church be able to meet the needs of a drifting, lost, and desperate world.

The Result of Being a Servant Leader

Many leaders have the mistaken idea that if they serve their followers, they will be viewed as weak and unfit for leadership. Such thinking couldn't be further from the truth. Servant leaders are *more* effective leaders than traditional leaders. A classic example of the results of *not* being a servant leader is found in 1 Kings 12. The chapter opens with Rehoboam, Solomon's son, being appointed king following Solomon's death. In verse 6 we see the new king consulting the elders who had served under Solomon and asking advice concerning how he should lead the people. The elders reply, "If today you will be a servant to these people and serve them and give them a favorable answer, they will always be your servants" (v. 7).

The elders were telling the new king to be a servant leader, but the king didn't like the idea of being a servant of the people. After all, he was a king—everyone knows a king should be served, not serve others. So King Rehoboam rejected the elders' advice and went to the young men he had grown up with to ask how to lead the people. Their advice was, "Tell these people who have said to you, 'Your father put a heavy yoke on us, but make our yoke lighter'—tell them, 'My little finger is thicker than my father's waist. My father laid on you a heavy yoke; I will make it even heavier. My father scourged you with whips; I will scourge you with scorpions" (vv. 10-11).

These young men were saying, "Use the power and control that goes with your position to force the people into line and make them serve you." That is exactly what Rehoboam tried to do. In short order, ten of the twelve tribes had rebelled because of Rehoboam's authoritative leadership style and had set up a separate nation under Jeroboam.

Some important lessons in leadership can be learned by studying 1 Kings 12. Like every other leader, King Rehoboam obviously wanted (and needed) the cooperation and support of his followers. The elders tried to teach him the key to successful leadership: If you will serve the needs of your followers, they in turn will serve your needs forever. However, like many leaders today, Rehoboam didn't like the idea of serving his followers. His position as king deserved more respect, so he used his power to try to control his followers and force them to serve him. He reaped the same result other leaders get when they attempt to force people into servitude—rebellion. Rehoboam lost most of his followers because of his authoritative style of leadership.

INSTEAD OF THE CHURCH LEADING THE BLIND, WE ARE COMING TO A TIME WHEN WE WILL INVITE THE BLIND TO LEAD THE CHURCH.

If you want to be an effective leader following biblical principles of leadership, commit yourself to serving the needs of your followers. In return your followers will serve your needs forever.

Meeting Needs

Jesus Christ told His disciples that if they wanted to be leaders in His kingdom, they could not follow the leadership practices of the secular community. They *must* serve their followers in the same way Jesus served His followers. The question must be asked, then, "What does it mean to be a servant leader?" In order to follow Jesus Christ's command we must answer that question.

A servant is one who meets the needs of the person he is serving. If it is a very hot day and you are thirsty, and I offer you a coat to wear, I haven't served you because I didn't meet your need. You need a cool, refreshing drink of water, not a coat. I am a servant only when I am meeting a need. Servant leaders see their job as meeting the needs of followers.

The secular community tends to say that followers should work for the leader, but Jesus Christ said the leader should be working for the followers. Secular leaders tend to use the power and authority of their positions to get the followers to serve their needs. On the other hand, servant leaders use power and authority to meet or serve the needs of followers as they work toward accomplishing the common goal of the group.

If you want to follow Jesus' command and be a servant leader, you first must learn what the needs of your followers are. You can't meet their needs unless you know them, and to know them you have to exert some energy. Once you know them, you can meet them. Jesus Christ spent most of the time during His ministry meeting the needs of others. He gave equal time to both beggar and rich man alike.

Chapter Summary
It is getting harder and harder to tell the difference between the way the church operates and the way the world operates. The church isn't losing ground today because its answers are no longer relevant. It's losing ground because it is copying a world that never had the answers in the first place. Instead of the church leading the blind, we are approaching a time when we will invite the blind to lead the church—with disastrous results.

The focal point of leadership is power. What the leader chooses to do with that power determines whether it is a positive or negative force. An effective leader is first an effective servant.

Personal Application
1. What are some of the reasons a leader may be reluctant to serve his or her followers in the following places:
   ● The home
   ● The church
   ● His or her group
   ● The job
2. Study Matthew 20:25-28.
   ● Why do some leaders tend to use their power to "lord it over," or control, their followers?
   ● What does that tell you about the leader?
   ● Make a list of the ways you intend to serve your followers more effectively in the four areas listed in question one. Keep a record of the results.

CHAPTER SEVEN

Learning to Lead with Love

Very few leaders and writers on the subject of leadership understand the importance of love in leadership. Jesus Christ not only understood the need to incorporate love into leadership, He made it a *requirement* for all who would become His followers and eventually go on to lead. Paul, one of the great leaders of the early church, clarifies for us the importance of love when he writes in this well-known passage from 1 Corinthians,

> If I had the gift of being able to speak in other languages without learning them, and could speak in every language there is in all of heaven and earth, but didn't love others, I would only be making noise. If I had the gift of prophecy and knew all about what is going to happen in the future, knew everything about *everything*, but didn't love others, what good would it do? Even if I had the gift of faith so that I could speak to a mountain and make it move, I would still be worth nothing at all without love. If I gave everything I have to poor people, and if I were burned alive for preaching the Gospel but didn't love others, it would be of no value whatever. (1 Cor. 13:1-3, TLB)

What a powerful statement concerning the importance of love! From Paul's statement, we must conclude that for leaders love is far more important than all the power they can generate.

In chapter 5 we pointed out the important role love plays in developing and maintaining unity in a group. In this chapter we will look at each of the characteristics of love and how the leader is to use them.

First Corinthians 13:4-8 gives a complete description of love. Let's look briefly at how each of these characteristics of love can be part of what leaders do.

Love Is Patient

Patience is a characteristic every leader needs. Most leaders, from time to time, pray, "Lord, give me patience with these people!" But some of them are actually thinking, *Lord, make the people stop irritating me!* Webster's *New World Dictionary* defines *patience* as "enduring pain, trouble, etc., with composure and without complaint. Calmly tolerating insult, delay, confusion, etc."

Patience means remaining calm if you are insulted by your followers, if work is not completed on time, and if there is confusion in carrying out instructions. That does not mean you put up with unconcern for deadlines, people who deliberately disobey instructions, or people who defy authority but that you do not retaliate by becoming angry and vengeful. You keep your emotions under control and remain calm.

Patience enables leaders to remain calm and levelheaded even during the most trying situations. Because it is an expression of love, patience is far more valuable than power when it comes to leading people.

Love Is Kind

When our followers try our patience, we are not only to remain calm (be patient), but we are to also be gentle with them. This is often difficult for leaders, who have the power to retaliate in many different ways, even to the point of removing people from the group.

As we discuss what love is, you will notice that we are actually discussing actions. It isn't enough to tell your followers that you love them, you must demonstrate it by your actions. Actions tell what is really in the heart.

Love Is Never Jealous or Envious

Jealous or envious leaders are dangerous. They resent the accomplishments of their followers and suspect their every action. If you harbor jealousy or envy toward your followers, you will very quickly destroy the effectiveness of your group or organization.

IT IS NEVER NECESSARY
FOR A LEADER TO BRAG
ABOUT ACCOMPLISHMENTS.
ACCOMPLISHMENTS SPEAK
FOR THE LEADER.

Jealousy causes the leader to lose sight of the cause or goal for which the group is striving. It creates mistrust and eventually hatred, the opposite of love. A jealous leader will try to destroy rather than build up followers. If you are harboring jealousy or envy toward any of your followers, you are not loving them, and if you are not loving them, you are disobeying a direct command of Jesus. You need to ask both Him and the person you envy to forgive you. Then you must change your actions.

Love Is Never Boastful or Proud

Boastfulness is a sign of selfishness. Boastful people are trying to draw attention to what they can do. Love never draws attention to self; it always promotes the other person. It is never necessary for a leader to brag about accomplishments. Accomplishments speak for the leader.

Effective leaders spend time encouraging and motivating their followers, and they work at helping the group develop the confidence to succeed. Boasting about your accomplishments not only indicates self-centeredness on your part, but it may also cause followers to feel less capable of success.

Love Is Never Haughty
Haughty means displaying pride in oneself while at the same time showing displeasure, contempt, and scorn for others. Christian leaders should never do anything to make their followers feel inferior. In the secular world, haughtiness is fairly common among leaders. It has no place among followers of Jesus Christ.

Jesus never acted as though He was better than His followers. He often acted as though they were better than He. Jesus took time for everyone, even the smallest of children. If you want to be an effective leader, guard against removing yourself from your followers and making them feel you think you are better than they are or that you are too good to do the things you ask them to do.

Love Is Never Selfish
It is easy for leaders to become selfish or self-centered. Being in charge of the group doesn't make your ideas better than those of your followers. Nor does it mean you are always right and they are always wrong when they disagree with you. Effective leaders work to promote their followers instead of themselves. That means that whenever possible, you use their ideas, opinions, and suggestions rather than your own. You also share your authority and power with those you are leading.

Love Is Never Rude
Selfishness and rudeness go hand in hand. When you are rude to another person, you are really saying by your actions, "I place much more value in my feelings and opinions than I do in yours."

The unfortunate thing about rudeness is that we often aren't even aware of it in ourselves. It is a sure sign that we are so caught up in ourselves that we have little if any concern for others. There is no place for rudeness in the life of a servant leader.

Love Does Not Demand Its Own Way
Because of their power, leaders can easily disguise the times they demand their own way. On many occasions I have listened to the suggestions of those I was leading but have done it my way even when their way may have been better.

As long as things have to be done your way, the group will never be able to go beyond your ability to make decisions. Your job as leader is not to always decide for the group, but to help develop their decision-making abilities. That means that whenever possible, things should be done their way instead of yours. Followers will learn to lead as they have opportunities to make decisions.

Love Is Not Irritable or Touchy
Are you grouchy, moody, or easily irritated? If you are, you are too self-centered. Irritation is a sign that we are focusing on what we want instead of focusing on serving others. The Bible says irritation is void of love. It goes along with impatience and intolerance, which are also unloving.

If you are easily irritated, moody, or grouchy, people will tend to avoid you. Your followers will not be willing to be open with you, because they will not trust you to be consistent. They will do only what they are told to do; rather than be creative, they will avoid taking risks.

Love Does Not Hold Grudges

Effective leaders must be very forgiving. Loving leaders not only forgive but forget. Grudges come from not forgiving people and harboring negative feelings toward people because of events in the past. We hold grudges because we feel wronged in some way and we want to get even.

Leaders who love their followers will overlook the times when they are wronged. The temptation is to repay evil for evil, but in order to demonstrate love we must be willing to repay evil with good. Holding grudges only leads to continuous conflict. Repaying evil with good defuses the conflict and opens the door to restoring harmony in the relationship.

Love Will Hardly Ever Notice When Others Do Wrong

What does this mean? As I thought about this characteristic of love, I was reminded of a boss I once had whom my coworkers and I had nicknamed "Snoopy," because he was always sneaking around trying to catch us doing something wrong. One day we spotted him watching us through a pair of field glasses, so we all waved and laughed at him. I never respected that boss.

Love trusts, respects, and believes in people. If I love you, I'm not looking for you to make a mistake. I am willing to overlook an occasional mistake, and when you make a mistake, I help you learn from it.

Love Is Never Glad about Injustice

Leaders who love their followers never get satisfaction from seeing them wronged. They don't play one person against another or deliberately set a person up to fail.

Effective leaders are committed to treating all of their followers equally and fairly. They don't show favoritism, nor are they willing to allow favoritism to exist in the group. If members of the group are mistreating one another, the loving leader is quick to deal with the issue impartially.

Love Rejoices When Truth Wins

Effective leaders are people of integrity. They can be counted on to operate from a position of truth, even to their own hurt. They require the same standards from their followers.

Loving leaders won't compromise their standards for the sake of personal gain, and they take the truths of the Bible as the final authority.

Love Is Loyal No Matter What the Cost

Loyalty is a rare commodity in our society today, but it is extremely important in a group if the group wants to survive the pressures working to weaken and eliminate it. If leaders want commitment from their followers, they must first demonstrate loyalty to them. Followers need to know that their leaders will stay with them through bad times and good times, that working with them is more important to their leaders than anything else, and that they are more important to their leaders than any other group.

Love Always Believes in the Other Person

If you want to demonstrate love to your followers, let them know that you believe in them, even when they don't believe in themselves. Never give up on their ability to reach their full potential. Challenge group members to believe in themselves, their potential, and the group's potential.

IF YOU EXPECT YOUR FOLLOWERS
TO GO OUT ON A LIMB FOR YOU,
THEN BE THERE TO CATCH THEM
WHEN IT BREAKS.

Believing in your followers means letting them use their creativity to better accomplish the goal or mission of the group. It means trusting their judgment and their decisions. It means continuing to believe in them when they make mistakes, and helping them turn those mistakes into positive learning experiences.

Love Always Defends the Other Person

Instead of promoting and defending self, love always promotes, protects, and defends the loved ones. That means that leaders defend their followers when others criticize them.

I once worked for a manager who encouraged me to try my ideas, but if they didn't work, he wouldn't defend me to his boss. After a while I was no longer willing to take the risks necessary to be innovative. If you expect your followers to go out on a limb for you, then be there to catch them when it breaks.

Love Goes On Forever

There is no end to love. That means you put love into action every day whether you feel like it or not. Even if your followers don't love you back, you keep on applying the principles of love. Love is never conditional; it doesn't depend on feelings or the response of the loved ones.

Chapter Summary

Putting love into action is not optional for the Christian leader who wants to follow New Testament principles of leadership. Jesus said, "A new command I give you: Love one another. As I have loved you, so you must love one another. By this all men will know that you are My disciples, if you love one another" (John 13:34-35).

I challenge you to make a commitment to consistently put into practice the actions of love described in 1 Corinthians 13:4-8. Because unless you do, all your power is of absolutely no value.

Personal Application

1. Study each of the characteristics of love listed in 1 Corinthians 13:4-8.
   - Which are you weakest in applying?
   - Which are you strongest in applying?
2. Develop an action plan to more effectively apply each of the characteristics.

CHAPTER EIGHT

Developing a Strong Team

It seems we do a lot of talking these days about the *team* concept of leadership. Very few leaders, however, actually understand how to effectively develop and lead a team. For example, I was asked by a large federal agency to train their group of middle managers in team dynamics and also assist in the process of developing several working teams at the middle-management level.

Before beginning the actual training, I conducted an organizational analysis to acquaint myself with their organizational structure and working processes. During this time I discovered that the people in top leadership positions felt that they were applying the team concept of leadership very effectively but that people at middle levels of leadership were not. As I talked with people at the middle levels, they assured me that people in top positions of leadership needed the training worse than those in the middle. As a result, we expanded the training to include both upper and middle management.

The Importance of Teams
Before a team can be developed, the leader must have a clear

understanding of what a team is. A team is not just a group of people assigned to one leader, manager, or department. A team is two or more people moving along a path of interaction toward a common goal. That definition has two important aspects. First, moving along a path of interaction requires effective communication. Second, team members have a common goal. They are all working for the same thing.

Ecclesiastes 4:9-12 gives us some reasons for teams.

Two can accomplish more than twice as much as one, for the results can be much better. If one falls, the other pulls him up; but if a man falls when he is alone, he's in trouble. Also, on a cold night, two under the same blanket gain warmth from each other, but how can one be warm alone? And one standing alone can be attacked and defeated, but two can stand back-to-back and conquer; three is even better, for a triple-braided cord is not easily broken. (TLB)

This passage contains some very important principles for teams. Let's examine them point by point.

Two people have the potential to accomplish more than twice as much as one working alone. If you have a group of followers all working individually on a project and transform them into a team, they will be much more productive. Two people working together as a team will be more productive than two people working separately.

Results are better when work is done as a team. A team not only accomplishes *more* work, but the work accomplished is also of *better* quality. There are several reasons for this. First, people tend to be more conscientious when they know their peers are watching. Second, when people have a common goal, they work harder individually because they know their failure can also cause the failure of their peers. There is a "one for all and all for one" spirit in a team. That is why we hear players of team sports say, "I don't care who gets the credit—I was just playing hard so we could win."

Team members are quick to help each other out of difficult situations. People working as individuals in a department or group cannot expect nearly as much help from their peers when they are in a difficult situation as when that same group is functioning as a team. In fact, group members working as individuals frequently work against one another as they individually compete for recognition. If one member of the group gets in trouble, the others may actually be glad to see that person's misfortune.

YOU CAN ALWAYS TELL WHEN YOU'VE DEVELOPED A TEAM. YOUR PEOPLE SAY "WE" INSTEAD OF "THEY."

On the other hand, if a group is working as a team, every individual on that team supports the others, because if one person fails or has difficulty it affects the entire team. For example, the field goal kicker on a football team isn't just kicking for his own success; he is kicking for the team. If he fails, it hurts the whole team. So the blockers on the line do their best to protect him, the center does his best to snap the ball perfectly, and the holder does his best to position the ball in exactly the right position. The whole team works to make the field goal kicker a success, and he kicks the ball to make the whole team a success. Rather than competition, there is cooperation.

Team Unity
As a management consultant I frequently have the opportunity to observe the lack of unity in organizations and groups—both secular and Christian. Anytime a leader complains to me about the lack of unity in his or her group or organization, I immediately know that the group members

aren't working as a team.

A team is unified because the group is pulling together for a common cause. They rely on one another, support one another, encourage one another, help one another, and protect one another, because they realize they need each other in order to accomplish their purpose. A team needs each individual in order to succeed.

A Common Goal

It isn't enough for a group to have goals. Every group has goals. In order for a group of followers to be a team, they must have a *common* goal. And there is a big difference between goals and a common goal. A common goal means it is the group's goal: they participated in its development; they have bought it emotionally and are committed to it. In other words, they *own* it.

A common goal creates group ownership. You can always tell when you've developed a team. Your people say "we" instead of "they." Have you ever noticed how often followers in a group or employees in a business refer to their organization as "they"? When you hear a follower do that, you know that he or she feels excluded from the part of the group that is responsible for making things happen. Team members, on the other hand, say "we" instead of "they," because they have a part in the goal setting and decision making of the organization.

One of the differences between a leader with a *group* of followers and a leader with a *team* of followers is that the *group* leader sets the goals for the group. The *team* leader gets the team involved in setting the goals. When that happens, the group begins to move from individual thinking to group thinking, on their way to being a team.

Ownership of the goal is one of the major differences between a group and a team. You cannot have a team if the leader sets all the goals. In order to put together a team, the leader must be willing to share some authority and decision-making power with followers. This is part of why so many leaders have a hard time actually developing a team—they aren't willing to share their power. If you aren't willing to share your power, don't complain about being overworked.

The sense of ownership that is generated when the leader gives the followers the power to help determine the group s goals is one of the most important but least understood aspects of team dynamics. As long as the leader sets the goals, followers have little to lose if they fail to meet the goals. But if the team is involved in setting the goals, they will do whatever it takes to succeed.

When the leader gives the team the responsibility for setting goals, "group thinking" results. The process of choosing a goal together creates a climate in which everyone is forced to provide input, consider pros and cons, and give and take until a consensus is reached. Group thinking creates much more momentum than individual thinking.

Even if the leader could have arrived at the same goal without the team's help, it would not generate energy in the group the way the group process can. Besides, a group of minds are much more capable of coming up with a good goal than a single mind.

Choosing the Right People

There are two key questions to be answered when choosing people for a team. This doesn't mean that other issues shouldn't be addressed, but if these two issues are properly addressed, in most cases the others can be easily worked out. The questions are *Are the candidate's personal goals compatible with the team's goals?* and *Will this person be able to effectively use his or her strengths to meet the team's goals?*

If the answer to either of these questions is no, that person will be frustrated, and that frustration will spill over into the team in the form of conflicts, lack of motivation, resentments, and ultimately, poor performance.

IF YOU AREN'T WILLING TO SHARE YOUR POWER, DON'T COMPLAIN ABOUT BEING OVERWORKED.

After graduating from seminary, Andrew Halstead served as a youth pastor for six years and then received an invitation to be the youth pastor for a very large church in Ohio. Andrew wanted to start his own church somewhere in the Northwest, but he finally agreed to join the ministry team of the church in Ohio.

From the very beginning he and his wife, Julie, were quite unhappy. Julie felt her gifts weren't needed, and Andrew felt like a small cog in only one wheel of a fast-moving train. He loved working with adults and starting something small and watching it grow.

But Andrew's new job involved maintaining an already successful program, and he had very little opportunity to start something from nothing. He and Julie quickly realized they had made a mistake in taking the job, but the church had gone to considerable expense moving them to the new city and helping them get established in a new home, so they felt obligated to stay.

Before long Andrew began developing severe tension headaches and had a great deal of trouble sleeping nights. His heart wasn't in his ministry, and it was hard for him to go to the church each day to do his work. He became disenchanted with the pastoral team and found himself struggling with depression. His performance was not up to the standards the church expected from its staff, and eighteen months after taking the job, he resigned at the request of the senior pastor. Andrew moved his family to the Northwest, got a job, and started a small Bible study in his home. The group grew, and today Andrew is the senior pastor of a church that began in the basement of his house and now has a congregation of over seven hundred people.

I recently had lunch with Andrew and Julie. Andrew commented, "You know, Myron, things are just running too smoothly. I'm getting the itch to start another Bible study group and watch it grow like this one has."

Andrew did not fit in well with the ministry team in Ohio, not because he lacked ability, but because his personal goals were so different from the goals of the ministry team there. Andrew's frustration led to frustration for the whole team. All of that could have been avoided if the team leader had made sure that the new minister of youth had personal goals compatible with the goals of the team and that his strengths fit the team's needs.

The Team Leader's Role

The team leader isn't just interested in putting together an effective team to accomplish a goal—any good leader can do that. The leader wants the team to achieve the goal, but he or she also must work with the individual team members to develop their leadership skills so that they in turn will be able to put together effective teams.

Team leaders need to create productive work environments, lead their teams in effective planning, be proficient in evaluating individual and team performance, and be good managers of time. Team leaders must be able to be members of the team while at the same time accepting ultimate responsibility for the team and its actions. To be a good team leader you must also be a good team player, so that the team works with you, not for you.

In order to work with your team, you must be vulnerable and transparent. Relax: your followers will discover your weaknesses whether you're open about them or not. They will respect you a lot more if you are candid about your limitations than if you try to appear to have all the answers to all the problems your followers could ever have. Don't let them put you on a pedestal.

TO BE A GOOD TEAM LEADER YOU MUST ALSO BE A GOOD TEAM PLAYER.

As the leader of your team your job is to help your followers reach their full potential. To do that, you must help them develop their strengths and overcome their weaknesses. Major on their strengths, not their weaknesses. People will always have weaknesses, and there will be other people who are strong where another is weak, so you can help team members compensate for one another's weaknesses. A team is most productive when each person is able to work in his or her area of strength. Your job is to help people find those areas and develop them to their potential. (You can find more information on the role of the leader in my *Management: A Biblical Approach*, published by Victor Books.)

Chapter Summary
A team is two or more people moving along a path of interaction toward a common goal. A team can not only accomplish more than the same number of people working alone, but also what they produce will be of higher quality. Unity around a common goal and team ownership of the goal foster high commitment among team members. Leaders need to know how to create teams.

Personal Application
1. Are you leading a group of followers or a team?
2. If your group is not already a team, what can you do to begin developing it into a team?
3. Work with the people in your group to identify their individual strengths and develop a plan to use those strengths more effectively.

CHAPTER NINE

The Art of Motivating Others

My son, Ron, played hockey while in high school and college. I will never forget one of his high school games. During the first two periods, he and his teammates played terribly. They seemed to be skating in slow motion; they weren't aggressive on either offense or defense and failed to score in either period.

However, after returning from the locker room following the end of the second period they seemed to be a totally different team. They outskated their opponents. They played aggressively, and they scored four goals to win by one point.

As I walked to the locker room following the game to congratulate the team and my son, who scored two of the goals, I thought about the big difference between the last part of the game and the first two periods. They were the same players; they had the same abilities; they were playing the same opponents. Yet there was no comparison between the way they played the first two periods and the way they played for the rest of the game.

I asked my son what had made the difference. He grinned and said, "We had a little talk among ourselves. For some reason we just weren't fired up at the beginning of the game, but we really got motivated before the third period and we came out and won it."

A leader will never be successful unless his or her followers are motivated to succeed. As Ron's high school hockey team demonstrated, it doesn't matter how much ability your followers have; if they aren't motivated, they will not perform up to their potential and reach their goal. Leaders must realize that one of their major functions is to help instill motivation in each of their followers.

Defining Motivation

Some of the most effective leaders are sometimes puzzled about how to help a person or group become motivated. After the hockey game I described, I also had an opportunity to talk to Ron's coach. When I asked him what his secret was to motivating his team so well, he said, "Myron, I wish I knew. If I did, we could package it and both get rich!"

While Ron took a shower and packed his hockey gear, his coach and I discussed how important motivation is in helping a team perform up to its potential. He said, "The amazing thing about motivation is that what works one time with one person or group won't necessarily work the next." He had been coaching high school students for over ten years. He pointed out that the mental preparation was just as important as skill building and physical preparation in sports.

What my son's coach had said was just as true concerning all of life. Motivation has to do with the mental preparation of the person or team. Most leaders know the importance of teaching followers the basics about their tasks, but all too many stop there and fail to help followers prepare mentally.

Motivation is *an inner drive that launches us into action*. The greater the motivation, the stronger the drive.

Principles of Motivation

Motivation must have a target. Motivation is always directed toward a specific action. The greater the motivation the stronger the drive to perform an action or achieve a goal. After Ron's hockey game he said, "For some reason we just weren't fired up at the beginning of the game." He didn't mean they didn't care about winning the game. If you had asked each player if he wanted to win the game, he would have said, "Of course!" He would have considered that a dumb question. But motivation always deals with our emotions.

Keep in mind that a goal will never become a reality without the proper level of motivation. It isn't enough to just set goals; many people set goals and never come close to accomplishing them. Each follower must be highly motivated to achieve the goals. In order for people to be motivated, they need to focus on a specific goal or action.

It is impossible for you to motivate anyone. You can't motivate another person. You can point out the need for motivation and help create the proper environment for motivation, but motivation comes from *within* each individual follower.

That does not mean leaders are never at fault when their followers lack motivation. Leaders almost always contribute to the lack of motivation in their groups. As a general rule, however, the more you try to *force-feed* motivation, the less motivated your followers will be.

A LEADER WILL NEVER BE SUCCESSFUL UNLESS HIS OR HER FOLLOWERS ARE MOTIVATED TO SUCCEED.

One summer I took a job as a door-to-door salesman. I loved meeting people, I believed in the product, and I enjoyed selling. But I hadn't learned how to handle it when people refused to buy the product. I took every refusal to buy as a personal rejection of me. My discouragement made my sales drop off drastically.

My sales manager knew very little—if anything—about motivation. As I grew more discouraged, he tried to cram motivation down my throat. He yelled at me and threatened to fire me. It only discouraged me more, and finally I quit. Later in my life I worked in sales again and learned that the fact that people don't buy something doesn't mean they are rejecting the salesperson. Once I had learned that, I not only enjoyed sales, but did quite well.

If my first sales manager had helped me learn that principle, I would have been motivated in my job and done very well in sales. By trying to force me to become motivated, he only contributed to my discouragement.

There is no set formula for motivation. My son's hockey coach was certainly right when he commented that what works one time with one person or group won't necessarily work the next. Even when working with a strong team, the leader must deal with each follower individually when considering the need for motivation. What motivates one person may or may not motivate another.

Goals and Motivation

Purpose is what motivates you to action, and the same can be said for goals. Purpose tells *why* I do what I do, and goals tell *what* I intend to do, *how much* I expect to do, and *when* I expect to have it done. Like the purpose, goals should play a major role in motivating us to action.

In order for goals to be motivational, as we saw in chapter 8, the followers must participate in the goal-setting process. But simply letting followers participate in goal setting is no guarantee that the goals developed will motivate your team or group.

In order for goals to be motivational they must: fulfill a need or desire; effectively use the follower's skills, gifts, and abilities; and be considered achievable.

From the leader's perspective, goals must be set at two

levels—first for the whole group, and then for each team member.

To be motivational, a goal must fulfill a need or desire. Leaders need to make sure goals help fulfill the needs and desires of the people who will carry out those goals. If someone is required to work toward a goal that doesn't meet his needs, it will tend to discourage instead of motivate him or her.

To be motivational, a goal must effectively use the follower's abilities. One of the reasons we have so many unmotivated people sitting quietly in the pews of our churches Sunday after Sunday but not getting involved is that we don't have enough Christian leaders in our churches dedicated to helping their congregations develop goals that use church members' abilities. Everyone needs to be needed and make a contribution.

A GOAL WILL NEVER BECOME A REALITY WITHOUT THE PROPER LEVEL OF MOTIVATION.

We must constantly remind ourselves that our churches don't exist for the benefit of our leaders; our leaders exist for the benefit of our churches. The Christian leader who uses the church as a platform to promote personal goals is no different from the Gentile leaders Jesus described in Matthew 20:25, who lord it over their followers. Too many leaders in the church use their followers to accomplish their own personal goals instead of serving their followers by helping them identify goals that will allow them to use their gifts. Our churches are filled with people with an abundance of talent that is untapped because no one has taken the time to uncover their talent and help them set goals to use that talent to contribute to the purpose of the church.

To be motivational, a goal must be achievable. As leaders

help followers set goals, they must make sure the goals are achievable. If standards and requirements are set too high they will only discourage group members. Consistently unachievable goals may cause followers to give up.

The Most Important Motivational Tool

Leaders operating on secular principles of leadership are limited to human ingenuity as they deal with the challenge of motivating followers. Christian leaders, however, have the most important and effective motivational tool known—the Bible. There are several things leaders should do from a biblical perspective to help followers become motivated.

Help them develop the right perspective on God and His power. Understanding the power of God that is available to us is an important key to personal motivation. Jeremiah wrote about God's power, "Ah, Sovereign Lord, You have made the heavens and the earth by Your great power and outstretched arm. Nothing is too hard for You" (Jer. 32:17). *Nothing is too hard for God!* Realizing this is a great source of motivation.

Ephesians 3:20 is one of my favorite verses describing the amount of God's power available to us, His children. "Now glory be to God who by His mighty power at work within us is able to do far more than we would ever dare to ask or even dream of—infinitely beyond our highest prayers, desires, thoughts, or hopes" (TLB). This great biblical truth has helped me stay motivated during some very difficult times in my life. I can speak from personal experience that having the right perspective of God and His power is a crucial key to motivation.

Help them understand their position with God. All too few Christians understand their relationship with God once they have invited Jesus Christ into their lives and accepted Him as their personal Lord and Saviour. Christians not only have their sins forgiven and receive eternal life, we are now God's children—part of His family. "For His Holy Spirit speaks to us deep in our hearts and tells us that we really are God's children. And since we are His children, we will share His treasures—for all God gives to His Son Jesus is now ours too. But if we are to share His glory, we must also share His suffering" (Rom. 8:16-17, TLB).

We are not only God's children; we also have the privilege of sharing His treasures. Over the years the truths presented in that passage have been a great motivating force in my life. This has been the basis for a positive self-image; it has provided a feeling of great personal security in the midst of a very insecure society; and it has motivated me to stronger trust and faith in God as my real Heavenly Father who views me as one of His own children.

If you are discouraged and unmotivated, I challenge you to spend time each day meditating on Ephesians 3:20 and Romans 8:16-17. You will be amazed at how the truths of these passages will motivate you to greater faith in God and positive actions in life's situations.

A Climate for Motivation

Leaders play an important role in motivating others because they are responsible for creating a climate in which motivation can occur. Let's look at some keys to creating that motivational environment.

Emphasize the importance of the cause. A group's cause is a very important motivator. It is what draws followers to leaders in the first place. It is what sparks their original enthusiasm. And it is the thing that will keep them going through hard and good times alike. Once your followers lose sight of the cause or purpose and no longer know why they do what they are doing, they won't care anymore. If we no longer know why we do what we do, we won't stay motivated.

That is why Jesus Christ continually emphasized His cause throughout His ministry. As He began His ministry, He challenged His disciples to join Him by saying, "Come, follow

Me . . and I will make you fishers of men" (Matt. 4:19). As He concluded His earthly ministry, He said, "Go and make disciples of all nations" (Matt. 28:19). From the beginning of His work with His disciples until He returned to heaven, Jesus never stopped emphasizing His purpose. His early followers took the Gospel throughout the known world in only a few short years—because they remained motivated by the cause.

If you are a leader with unmotivated followers, you need to place greater emphasis on your cause and its importance. As you do, you will see higher levels of motivation among your followers.

Let your followers know they are important and needed. Jesus Christ was a master at letting His followers know their importance and how much He needed them in accomplishing the purpose. He told His followers, "You are the salt of the earth" and "You are the light of the world" (Matt. 5:13-14). He wasn't talking about Himself, but them.

Jesus' appreciation of His followers is one of the things that made Him a great leader. He never promoted Himself at His followers' expense. He continually encouraged them and supported them. He once told His disciples, "Anyone who has faith in Me will do what I have been doing. He will do even greater things than these, because I am going to the Father" (John 14:12).

What a powerfully motivating statement! Every time I read that verse, I am reminded of my junior high basketball coach. I was always impressed with his ability to play basketball and how well he knew the game. One day during practice he put his arm on my shoulder and said, "If you keep practicing, someday you'll be able to play better than me." I will never forget the impact that had on me. I thought, *Wow! If I could someday be a better player than my coach by just practicing hard enough, then I'm sure going to keep practicing!* Similar things must have been going through the minds of Jesus' disciples when He told them that.

Do you want motivated followers? Let them know how

important they are.

Focus on their strengths instead of their weaknesses. People get the greatest satisfaction out of their work and are the most motivated when they are working in their areas of strength rather than weakness. Leaders who want to create a climate for motivation should always capitalize on their followers' strengths rather than their weaknesses. The followers will not only be more motivated, but more productive as well.

Dr. Samuel Bradberry worked as a cross-cultural preparedness counselor for a missions organization. He had held the position for over ten years, and everyone in the organization recognized him as an excellent cross-cultural counselor, highly skilled in preparing missionaries for new assignments in different cultures.

Because of his effectiveness he was offered and he accepted an administrative position in the organization. I first met Dr. Bradberry at a management seminar I was holding for his organization. During a lunch break he told me, "They sent me to this seminar to try to make a manager out of me, but I think it's hopeless." As we talked, I discovered he was a frustrated and discouraged man. He had loved his work as a cross-cultural counselor and had been very effective, but he was a poor administrator and didn't enjoy the responsibilities and duties of his new position.

Fortunately, Dr. Bradberry's supervisor recognized the mistake and helped arrange for him to return to his former position. He later told me, "If they hadn't transferred me back to counseling I probably would have eventually left the organization. I'm just not cut out to be an administrator."

Dr. Bradberry's supervisor was a very wise leader. He knew that a person was more motivated and productive when allowed to focus on his personal strengths and was willing to help him return to his former position where he could make the greatest contribution and be the most satisfied in his work.

Always attack the problem, not the person. Another important element in creating a climate for motivation is to attack problems, not people. If a follower makes a mistake or performs poorly, deal with the mistake or performance problem, but don't attack the person.

Focus on the objective aspects of a team member's poor performance; don't attack his or her personal character. Such a character attack (for example, accusing the person of laziness) will only put him or her on the defensive. Dealing with the problem leads to positive results; attacking someone's character only leads to conflict and decreased motivation.

WE MUST CONSTANTLY REMIND OURSELVES THAT OUR CHURCHES DON'T EXIST FOR THE BENEFIT OF OUR LEADERS; OUR LEADERS EXIST FOR THE BENEFIT OF OUR CHURCHES.

Give proper recognition. Proper recognition includes both praise for a job well done and constructive criticism when needed. The Parable of the Talents in Matthew 25 provides an excellent description of the principles for providing proper recognition. In this parable the master went on a long journey and left his servants in charge of his resources. When he returned he gave praise, promotion, and increased monetary rewards to the two servants that had been productive, and he provided constructive criticism for the one that had been unproductive and fired him.

Jesus Christ gave both praise and constructive criticism as it was needed. In Luke 10:38-42 we see Jesus providing constructive criticism to Martha for being bogged down in busywork and praising Mary, her sister, for having the right priorities.

Here are some guidelines for constructive criticism:

- Don't just criticize; offer encouragement for improvement.
- Don't tell someone how to solve the problem until you first provide him or her an opportunity to suggest a solution.
- Once the solution has been determined, let the person try again in order to correct his mistake.
- Once the mistake has been corrected, be sure to praise the person involved.

Chapter Summary
Motivation is one of the most important, yet least understood, ingredients for success. It is that inner drive that launches us into action. Leaders can't motivate followers, but as they apply the principles outlined in this chapter they will begin to foster a climate in which motivation can occur.

Personal Application
1. How would you evaluate the motivation level of your followers? Is it improving or deteriorating? Why?
2. As you evaluate your group's goals, do you feel they effectively motivate your followers? Why or why not?
3. How could you better use the gifts of the people in your group?
4. How could you more effectively use God's Word to help motivate your followers?
5. How can you better emphasize the importance of your purpose?
6. Identify ways in which you will let your followers know that they are important and needed.
7. How can you better focus on the strengths of your people?
8. What will you do to give proper recognition to your followers?

CHAPTER TEN

Recruiting and Leading Volunteers

The lack of volunteers is one of the greatest tragedies in the church today. In fact, there are so few true volunteers in the modern church that we probably need to remind ourselves what a volunteer is: a person who by his own initiative and free will steps forward to perform a task. Such persons are so rare in Christendom today that most Christian leaders go into temporary shock when approached by one.

A Christian leader from a large denomination once said to me with a smile, "I agree it usually takes some strong urging and persuading, but we seem to be able to get people to volunteer." Such people are not volunteers. When the church has to start pleading with its people for help, it no longer has volunteers but a manipulated work force.

A Warning Sign
The lack of volunteers in the church today is a sign that we have lost sight of our cause. When you lose sight of the cause, you are no longer committed to it. We have lost our commitment to the cause. For most modern Christians, Christianity is not a cause worth fighting for. It doesn't even deserve our spare time. At numerous points in this book I

have indicated how important one's cause or purpose is in leadership. It is especially important to recruiting and leading volunteers.

One of the reasons people in church congregations fail to volunteer is that they see their roles as that of observers not workers. Once they have "voluntarily" attended the Sunday morning church service to observe the performance, they feel they have met their obligation and fulfilled their role. They have added to the number of observers in attendance and provided a listening audience for the performers.

WHEN THE CHURCH HAS TO PLEAD WITH ITS PEOPLE FOR HELP, IT NO LONGER HAS VOLUNTEERS BUT A MANIPULATED WORK FORCE.

It's not really fair to criticize them too harshly for performing this role. After all, in many cases, this is the role model they have had for years. Their parents and grandparents before them probably did the same thing, because their leaders encouraged it. Our Christian leaders have been willing to settle for a church full of observers instead of a congregation of workers because our modern religious system requires it.

This religious system places tremendous pressure on our full-time, "professional" Christian leaders to succeed. For the past several decades Christendom has been steadily moving toward the current ideal of the "superchurch." The superchurch, with its giant, modern facilities, large congregations, multifaceted programs, and its Sunday morning worship services beamed across the nation on radio and television airways, has become the model of success most churches and their leaders are striving for. While I do not criticize our large churches and their programs, I am very disturbed by the success symbol they have become within

American Christianity.

This superchurch success syndrome forces the leaders of the church to focus on filling up the seats and providing the audience of viewers with a professional performance, because that is what is expected in order to climb the career ladder. The Christian leader's success is frequently measured in terms of the size of the congregation and the number of programs offered for members' "religious entertainment." Church leaders are expected to offer seminars and workshops, write books, and go on speaking tours to enlighten other seekers of success with their secrets for climbing the religious system's ladder of success. The only support they need is financial support, so the "professionals" can develop the best religious entertainment and attract even more observers to watch the show. The end result is churches full of people who come to be entertained, not to help do the work, and a small group of leaders slowly burning themselves out under the responsibility and pressure of trying to provide a better and better performance for the audience.

We are desperately in need of a new kind of leader—one who puts getting the Gospel of Jesus Christ to a lost and hurting world above playing the political and religious games necessary for achieving our religious system's ideal of success. We desperately need leaders who not only know how to recruit people to the cause of Jesus Christ, but also know what to do with them once they volunteer. As long as our Christian leaders continue to see their primary roles as performers, our church congregations will continue to consist of people who come only to watch a performance.

Right Attitudes for Recruiters

Many leaders have trouble recruiting and leading volunteers because they have the wrong attitude. In order to be effective, Christian leaders need to make sure they have the right attitudes.

Recognize the need for help. This is the first attitude that must be developed. It may seem obvious, but I am amazed at how many Christian leaders try to do all the work themselves. There are many reasons for this.

Some leaders feel they are the only ones in the group or organization qualified to do the job. Others feel they are expected to do all the work because of their position. Still others are reluctant to let people know they need help for fear their followers will see their need as weakness. And even though they wouldn't admit it, some leaders simply don't want to give up any of the power of their position by letting others become involved. All these reasons indicate a lack of leadership maturity.

WE DESPERATELY NEED LEADERS WHO NOT ONLY KNOW HOW TO RECRUIT PEOPLE TO THE CAUSE OF JESUS CHRIST BUT ALSO KNOW WHAT TO DO WITH THEM ONCE THEY VOLUNTEER.

I recently attended a church pastored by a friend of mine. He mowed the church lawn on Saturday, taught the adult Sunday School class, was the official greeter on Sunday morning, handed out the bulletins, gave the opening welcoming remarks, led the congregational singing, made all the announcements, prayed all the prayers in the service, sang a special song with his wife, preached the sermon, and greeted the people as they left the service. It's no wonder a fourth of his congregation slept through his sermons!

If you're going to recruit volunteers, you must first recognize your need for help. I wasn't surprised that when my pastor friend announced a special church cleanup day one Saturday, only one person showed up.

Recognize that God has given everyone a special gift or ability for building up the body of Christ. Leaders must strongly believe Ephesians 4:11-12:

Some of us have been given special ability as apostles; to others He has given the gift of being able to preach well; some have special ability in winning people to Christ, helping them to trust Him as their Saviour; still others have a gift for caring for God's people as a shepherd does his sheep, leading and teaching them in the ways of God. Why is it that He gives us these special abilities to do certain things best? It is that God's people will be equipped to do better work for Him, building up the church, the body of Christ, to a position of strength and maturity." (TLB)

This passage makes it very clear that God has given each of us a special ability to be used in helping others in the church. God never intended for a few leaders to do all the work in the church. He expects everyone to be involved in helping each other. The leader's job is to make sure that happens.

Why Do People Volunteer?
Leaders need to understand why people volunteer. Most Veterans Administration hospitals have very effective volunteer programs. A few years ago I had the privilege of observing one of these programs in action while providing management consulting services for a Veterans Administration hospital.

THE MORE IMPORTANCE YOU PLACE ON THE JOB, THE MORE PEOPLE WILL BE WILLING TO DO THE JOB.

Over a period of several months I spent many hours with the administrator of the hospital's volunteer program and was amazed at the number of people doing very important jobs for no pay. Volunteers performed tasks ranging from answering questions at information booths to serving as medical doctors on various projects—all without pay!

I asked the program administrator to explain how she was able to get so many different people to volunteer their time and talents. She said, "You have to realize how strongly people need to feel *needed.*" She explained that one of the keys to recruiting and keeping volunteers was effectively communicating the *importance* of the job to be performed. She said, "The more importance you place on the job, the more people will be willing to do the job."

She pointed out that most people being paid for their work don't really feel appreciated or needed. They know that if they quit today they can be replaced tomorrow, yet we all need to feel needed and appreciated. She said, "When I interview prospective volunteers, the first thing I do is let them know how important the job is they are being considered for. Next, I tell them how grateful I am that they have the skills needed to perform the task and are willing to use those skills to perform such an important job for us. And then I let them know how much people like them are needed and appreciated in our volunteer organization." She laughed and continued, "By that time, they would do almost anything for the opportunity to do the job because they need to be needed and appreciated."

I learned some very important lessons that day concerning why people volunteer. All of us do have a great need to feel needed. We want the satisfaction of knowing that what we are doing is important and greatly appreciated. For years industrial psychologists have been telling us that feeling appreciated is far more important to employees than the amount of money they make. This woman confirmed that. She said, "My biggest problem isn't finding enough volunteers to fill our jobs; it's finding enough meaningful jobs for all our volunteers."

I left her office that day with those words ringing in my ears. As I walked down the hall of that hospital I was reminded of the countless church leaders who had complained to me about the lack of volunteers in their churches.

Most of us could learn a valuable lesson from the administrator of that volunteer program. We need to understand that people will stand in line to volunteer for a job if they are aware of its importance and know they are needed and appreciated when they offer to perform the tasks.

Recruiting Volunteers

Before you can lead volunteers, you must first recruit them. The effective leader is also an effective recruiter. Let's look at a few pointers for effective recruiting.

Communicate the importance of the job. Failure to communicate the importance of the job is one of the biggest mistakes church leaders make when trying to recruit volunteers. For example, during a management seminar I was conducting, the Christian education director of a large church complained about the dearth of teachers in their Sunday School program. When one pastor asked him how he recruited teachers, he said, "I usually make regular announcements in the bulletin and from the pulpit telling people we need teachers. If they are interested they are to see me following the service."

As I discussed the problem further with him during a break I discovered he was doing nothing to let people know how important the teaching positions were in the overall ministry of the church. He was focusing on the importance of filling the position, but he wasn't communicating the importance of the job itself. To potential volunteers, a vacant job usually indicates a job that is not very rewarding, so stressing the importance of filling the job only reinforces those suspicions.

Emphasize the importance of the position and the contribution it is making to building up the body of Christ and advancing the kingdom of God. Every job in the church should be evaluated in these terms; then as you recruit people to fill those jobs, you will be prepared to explain each job's importance.

For example, which of these jobs would you be most interested in?

1. We need people to volunteer to work in the nursery as baby-sitters during the morning worship service to provide a break for the parents.
2. We need people to volunteer to serve in the nursery during the morning worship service, caring for infants and toddlers and teaching them basic principles about God and His love. In this very important position you will be helping mold children's lives and influence them for God. You will also play a major role in helping create a worshipful atmosphere during the morning service and help make it possible for more parents to learn and grow in their personal walk with Jesus Christ. Because of the very important nature of this position, only those who have a sincere love for small children and want to have an important part in creating a worshipful service need apply.

All too many church leaders take an approach similar to the first one when recruiting volunteers. Once the importance of the task is communicated, you will discover that people will be much more interested in donating their time, energy, and talents because they want to make an important contribution to God and His work.

Let people know the job can't be done without them. One of the biggest mistakes Christian leaders make is doing jobs *for* the people instead of *with* them. As long as leaders will do the work for the people, they will feel no need to volunteer.

Doug and Shirley Albright, friends of mine, have two teenage children. One evening at a party at the Albrights' home Doug said, "I wish our kids were more interested in the youth group at church. Our poor youth minister is knocking himself out trying to develop a good program for the kids at church, but all they do is complain."

Doug and Shirley explained that their youth minister planned a special activity for the young people every Sunday evening after church. Shirley said, "Last Sunday evening he had them over to his house for games and pizza, and our kids came home griping about the boring games and awful pizza." I suggested that they meet with the youth pastor and suggest that he get the young people more involved in planning and carrying out the youth functions, and they followed my suggestion.

A few months later Doug and Shirley told me that things were going much better with the youth program. The youth pastor had given the young people the responsibility for planning the weekly after-church parties, and they had come up with some activities everyone seemed to enjoy.

As long as the youth pastor did everything for the young people, they didn't feel needed. When he turned the planning over to the youth, they suddenly realized that if there were going to be after-church parties, they were going to have to organize them. This was the motivation they needed to create events that were meaningful and of interest to them. The kids got involved and the pastor had more time to do other things for them.

Let people know how much you appreciate their skills and willingness to use them. If you want people to volunteer, let them know you believe in their ability to do the job. Focus on their skills and how they are needed to perform the task at hand. One of the major reasons people fail to volunteer is that they think, *I'm not qualified to do that!*

Once you find a person with the qualifications to do the job, let him or her know they are qualified and that you respect their willingness to do the job.

Keeping Volunteers
By virtue of their dynamic personalities, some leaders are able to recruit volunteers but don't know what to do with

them after they have them.

Maintain high performance standards. There is no value in emphasizing to a prospective volunteer how important a job is if you don't maintain high performance standards once the person volunteers to do the job. The veterans hospital's volunteer program director told me, "We actually maintain higher performance standards for our volunteers than for our full-time paid employees and we let our volunteers know the standards are higher."

That was one of the ways they let the volunteers know how important their jobs were. She said, "The results have been amazing! Our volunteers take more pride in their work than many of our paid personnel. They do better work, and as a result, we have some jobs that we will only let volunteers do." As a result of the high performance standards the volunteers didn't feel like second-class citizens but like an elite group of professionals.

I had an opportunity to speak at length with many people in that volunteer program, and they were excited about and proud of their work. One reason for their enthusiasm was the high expectations set by the director of the program.

Jesus Christ had high standards for those who volunteered to follow Him. "Anyone who loves his father or mother more than Me is not worthy of Me; anyone who loves his son or daughter more than Me is not worthy of Me; and anyone who does not take his cross and follow Me is not worthy of Me" (Matt. 10:37-38). Paul writes, "Whatever you do, work at it with all your heart, as working for the Lord, not for men" (Col. 3:23).

PROGRAMS ARE NEVER SUCCESSFUL— PEOPLE ARE.

I have observed, however, that performance standards are generally lower in Christian organizations than in other groups. In the name of love and understanding people in Christian organizations are allowed to get away with poor performance that would cost them their jobs in secular organizations.

There is no excuse for low performance standards among Christians. We have the greatest cause and purpose in the world. We have the power of God backing our mission and work. We are commanded to do our jobs as though we are working directly for the Lord. What else do we need to motivate us to high standards of performance?

I have had many church leaders tell me, "We can't expect as much from our people as other organizations do because our positions are filled by volunteers." Satan loves that excuse. He certainly doesn't want Christian leaders to expect much from their followers.

Setting high performance standards and seeing that they are met is one of the best ways to keep volunteers once you have recruited them because they indicate the importance of the job. On the other hand, the attitude that says, "Since you're a volunteer, anything you can do will be appreciated," which is displayed by so many church leaders, is one of the surest ways to discourage volunteers. They realize that their jobs aren't all that important.

Make heroes out of your volunteers. Publicly let volunteers and others around them know how much you appreciate them, what a good job they are doing, and that you couldn't have gotten it done without them. This will go a long way toward keeping volunteers motivated to continue their fine performance and also help motivate others to volunteer.

The hospital volunteer program director writes a monthly article for the local newspaper describing volunteers and their various projects. She chooses a volunteer of the month and has his or her picture in the paper with the article. The hospital puts on a monthly luncheon for the volunteers, where they receive awards and public recognition for the fine work they are doing.

Tailor your programs to the people, not the people to the programs. One of the biggest mistakes church leaders make is to allow programs to become sacred cows and to try to make new volunteers fit into the mold of old programs.

Volunteers need to use their gifts and abilities, so you need to find out what those gifts and abilities are and design your programs around those. Keep in mind that new volunteers won't be motivated to work on a project that was designed around the skills of previous volunteers.

Most leaders make the mistake of expecting their volunteers to be flexible and fit into their rigid programs. Just the opposite should be true. Leaders should be flexible, able to mold programs around the talents of volunteers. Programs are never successful—people are. Leaders need to help volunteers be as successful as possible because the more successful the volunteers are, the longer they will offer their services. Always think in terms of the success of the people, not the success of the programs. Successful people make programs a success.

Chapter Summary
A volunteer is a person who on his or her initiative performs a task. Our lack of volunteers is one of the greatest tragedies in the church today, and we need to see it as the warning sign that it is. Have we lost our commitment to the cause?

Personal Application
1. Why do we lack volunteers in the church?
2. Evaluate your skills in recruiting volunteers. Where do you need improvement?
3. Evaluate your skills in leading volunteers. How could you improve?

CHAPTER ELEVEN

Making Leaders Out of Followers

The Christian church is in a war, a war against "persons without bodies—the evil rulers of the unseen world, those mighty satanic beings and great evil princes of darkness who rule this world; and against huge numbers of wicked spirits in the spirit world" (Eph. 6:12, TLB). To win the war, the church desperately needs more godly leaders willing to let God work His power through them against the forces of evil. If we are to regain our strength, we need new leaders—leaders who know how to turn followers into leaders.

As I have emphasized throughout the book, the new leader must do more than point the way for others to follow. Traditional leaders have been doing that for years, and the church has been steadily losing ground using that approach to leadership. The new leaders must not only point the way for others to follow, they must also be able to train followers to be effective leaders.

The emphasis of traditional leadership has been on teaching followers truths, facts, and principles. Therefore, most formal training focused on preparing leaders to be teachers and speakers. However, there is a big difference between teaching and training. The teacher's job is finished once he or she has imparted the information, but new leaders must realize that teaching the information is only the first step. After they present the information, their most important task begins—that of training followers in the application of that information.

Training is the transformation of information into application. Until recently only highly motivated churchgoers have moved from teaching to application—and then usually on their own. Such people are few and far between. They figured out how to apply information in spite of their leaders, not because their leaders trained them in application.

Training in application must become the norm in the church. Our leaders must learn how to not only teach, but also train their followers in application. This is the road to turning followers into leaders.

The new leader will adopt the leadership principles and practices used by Jesus Christ. Jesus Christ said, "Follow Me . . . and I will make you fishers of men" (Matt. 4:19). Traditional Christian leaders say, "Follow me, and we will talk about the need to fish for men." Leadership in the church too often focuses on *what*; New Testament principles of leadership focus on *how*. Leaders must be able to train followers in making practical application of the truth.

Get Involved!

The secret to turning followers into leaders is *involvement*. Unfortunately the church is one of the most uninvolved groups of people in our society. Week after week, month after month, and year after year Christians meet in their churches to watch a handful of their peers do all the work. We must begin recognizing that followers become leaders by doing, not just watching.

Jesus knew His followers would never become effective leaders just by watching Him do His work, so He got them involved. "When Jesus had called the Twelve together, He gave them power and authority to drive out all demons and to cure diseases, and He sent them out to preach the kingdom of God and to heal the sick" (Luke 9:1-2). Then in the next chapter we see Him getting even more of His followers involved with Him in His ministry. "After this the Lord appointed seventy-two others and sent them two by two ahead of Him to every town and place where He was about to go. He told them, 'The harvest is plentiful, but the workers are few. Ask the Lord of the harvest, therefore, to send out workers into His harvest field' " (Luke 10:1-2).

> ## A LEADER'S JOB IS NOT COMPLETED UNTIL HIS FOLLOWERS HAVE TAKEN HIS PLACE.

Jesus didn't just involve His followers in busywork. He got them directly involved in doing what He was doing. This is extremely important. In chapter 1 we redefined leadership as recruiting people to follow one's example and guiding them along the way while training them to do what the leader does. By definition new leaders must focus on getting followers involved in what they are doing.

Five Levels of Involvement

There are five steps for turning followers into leaders. With each step, the follower has more authority, and the leader has less. The leader should explain the five levels of involvement to followers and let them know that there is no set timetable for the process. Some followers will move through the five steps more quickly than others, depending on their background, experience, and ability.

Emphasize that you are a team; the team's goal is to help one another not only be good followers, but also develop into effective leaders. It is also important to point out that your primary role as the team leader will be to provide the

STEP ONE	STEP TWO	STEP THREE	STEP FOUR	STEP FIVE
The follower carries out the leader's instructions.	The follower carries out the leader's instructions, but the leader asks for the follower's input.	The leader assigns the follower the task of designing and carrying out a project with input from the leader. The leader assigns others to be led by the follower.	The follower designs and carries out a project without input from the leader. The follower suggests to the leader who should work under him or her in the project. The leader evaluates the results with the follower.	The follower puts together his or her own team of followers and works independently of the leader, except for input as needed and occasional evaluation. At some point the follower becomes totally independent of the leader and begins this process with his or her own followers.

The five levels of involvement.

support they need in order to become effective leaders. You are their resource person and servant as they work at developing their leadership skills.

STEP ONE. During the first step the emphasis is on becoming a good follower. Followers will never become effective leaders until they learn to be good followers. During this first step followers must learn three things.

The importance of following instructions properly. During this first phase of followers' development into leaders you must instill in them how important it is to follow instructions properly if the group is to accomplish its purpose. It is important for leaders to provide clear instructions on all assignments and then evaluate how well they are being followed. Don't move a follower to step 2 until you are satisfied he or she knows how to follow instructions.

During this first stage encourage followers to ask questions. This first level is a learning period; there is no such thing as a "dumb" question. It is far better to ask questions ahead of time than to make a mistake and then ask.

Necessary basic skills. This is a time of learning for the follower. Leaders need to make sure followers know how to perform the various tasks required.

The importance of serving others. From the very beginning leaders must emphasize the biblical approach to leadership not only by talking about it but also by modeling it. If we don't learn to serve as followers, we certainly won't as leaders.

STEP TWO. At this phase of a follower's development into a leader, the leader begins asking for the follower's input in the decision-making process. The leader still makes the decisions, but not until the followers have had an opportunity to provide input. Leaders should evaluate followers' input because it is an important indicator of how well they grasp the situation. The input helps the leader determine when a follower is ready to handle the increased responsibility of designing and carrying out a project with input from the leader.

STEP THREE. This is a major step forward in a follower's development into a leader. At this point the leader turns over to the follower the responsibility for designing and carrying out a project, with input as needed from the leader. The leader also assigns other followers to work under the supervision and leadership of the person being moved to step three.

This is a very important step for both the follower and the leader. The follower is beginning to draw on all the things he or she has learned about the various aspects of leadership up to this point and is applying them for the first time in an actual leadership role. The leader must carefully evaluate the follower's performance.

It is very important that the leader be more of a "coach" than a leader to the follower. Followers at this step must take responsibility for the project, including leading their assistants. Leaders should be available as consultants when needed. Leaders should clarify the amount of decision-making power followers will have and make it clear to all that they have veto power over all decisions made by the followers.

Leaders should serve as close observers of the project and evaluate followers' leadership.

STEP FOUR. Once the leader is satisfied with a follower's capability to design and carry out a project and effectively lead others, he or she moves the follower to the next phase of development. During the fourth step the follower becomes an actual peer with the leader. The leader's role is limited primarily to making final approvals and being available for consultation if needed. The leader no longer maintains regular contact with the details of the operation.

At this point the leader has placed total confidence in the follower as a leader. The follower is a fellow leader and has all the authority necessary for getting the job done. At the end of the project the leader and the follower will evaluate the results together.

STEP FIVE. The follower is now a leader in his own right, ready to recruit a team of followers independent of the leader's group. This is frequently a very difficult time for both followers and leaders because of the strong emotional ties that frequently develop between them. However, leaders must insist that followers launch out on their own. Failure to do so will limit followers and hinder leaders from training new followers.

THE STAKES HAVE NEVER BEEN HIGHER, NOR THE APATHY GREATER THAN IN THE CHURCH TODAY.

During the early phases of this step the leader will continue to maintain occasional contact, offering advice when needed; however, at some point the leader will probably be seeking as much advice from the former follower as he or she is giving. Such leaders will then have the satisfaction of knowing they have truly reproduced themselves as leaders, fulfilling the real purpose of leadership.

A leader's greatness isn't measured by what he can do—but what his former followers can do. Jesus Christ was not a great leader because He could perform great miracles and many people wanted to follow Him. He was a great leader because His followers achieved great things for God. A leader's success is always measured in terms of the level of achievement of his followers. If you want to become a better leader, work at helping your followers achieve their full potential.

Chapter Summary

The church is desperately in need of more godly leaders if we are to fulfill the command of taking the Gospel to a lost and hurting world. New leaders must not only be able to help people grow in their walk with Jesus Christ, they must also know how to turn their followers into leaders like themselves.

As I write the concluding comments of this book, I can't help but wonder what will be going through the minds of those who will read this far. At times I have made some strong statements concerning the ineffectiveness of the church, and I have placed most of the blame on our traditional approach to leadership. You can judge whether those charges are accurate. I approach the subject of Christian leadership from the point of view of a management consultant who also happens to be a Christian. You must approach your evaluation from your perspective.

If at times I have sounded like an alarmist, it is because as a professional in the area of organizational dynamics I am very alarmed at what I see happening (and not happening) in the church. The stakes have never been higher nor the apathy greater than in Christendom today. If the church expects to be a positive force, with solutions to the problems and remedies for the ills of humanity during the next century, it must awaken from its slumber and begin training an army of Christian leaders committed to the principles and practices of leadership taught and applied by Jesus Christ.

Satan is determined to destroy the church's ability to serve as the light marking the path to God in our dark and lost world. He knows that he must make its leaders ineffective, because an organization is only as strong as its leaders.

Christendom at the Crossroads

Today our leaders stand at a crossroad. They can choose to follow the ways of the past and continue practicing the traditional approach to leadership, which overworks them and makes unproductive spectators out of their followers. Or they can choose to apply Jesus Christ's principles of leadership, which make effective leaders out offollowers.

To continue with the traditional approach would decrease the church's effectiveness in reaching the world with the Gospel. To choose to implement New Testament principles of leadership would cause the trauma of breaking with long-standing traditions, but it would also ensure an effective, productive army of Christian leaders to minister to a lost world and provide hope for the future as we approach and enter the twenty-first century.

Every Christian must choose which road to travel. Which way will you choose? The world is waiting for your answer.

Personal Application

1. Study the five steps of increasing involvement and begin developing your own plan of action for turning your followers into leaders.
2. Go through this book with your followers and have them complete the personal application projects at the end of each chapter as you begin working with them in the five-step leadership development plan.

APPENDIX

There is no value in my pointing out the need to turn followers into leaders unless I am also willing to provide some tools for doing so. For the past several years I have been designing and conducting management and leadership development programs for a wide variety of Christian groups and organizations. The following projects and exercises are tools I have found helpful in fostering leadership skills in others.

Each exercise may be modified to fit the specific needs of your group, so feel free to experiment with them. Since an individual learns to be a leader by doing, most of the exercises are designed to maximize involvement on the part of group members.[1]

I would be interested in hearing from you concerning the results of these projects and exercises and any suggestions you might have for how they might be improved.

1. You may reproduce any portion of this section for training purposes. No part of this section, however, may be reproduced for resale.

COLLECTING GROUP INPUT ON GROUP GOALS
Goals:
- To involve group members in providing input into the goal-setting process for the team or group.
- To provide an opportunity for the group to interact concerning the group's goals.
- To foster a spirit of unity around the group's goals.

Group size:
Unlimited. If the group is large, divide into smaller groups of 5–6 people.

Time required:
Approximately 1 hour, depending on the size of the group.

Physical setting:
A space large enough for the entire group to meet together in a general session and spaces for small-group meeting sessions. In the large meeting space chairs should be provided for people, arranged in a circle if possible. Tables should be provided in the small-group meeting areas.

Materials needed:
Newsprint and marking pen for each small group
Several sheets of paper
Pencils
Masking tape

Procedure:
1. In a large group take about five minutes to explain the importance of goal setting and the need for everyone's input. Explain that the suggestions for goals should be stated in terms of *what* is to be accomplished, *how much* is to be accomplished, and *by when* it is to be accomplished. Then break the large group into small groups.
2. Have small groups each select someone to record group members' suggestions. Have each small group take

5–10 minutes to discuss goals for your team or organization. Then have each person write down what he or she feels the group's goals should include. After about 10 minutes have each person report his or her ideas. (The recorder should write them on the newsprint.)

3. Regather the large group and collect their newsprint sheets. Review the goal suggestions from the small groups with the entire group. Thank the group for their valuable input and let them know that the information will be used in determining the group's goals.

4. Using group members' ideas and the assistance of any group members, set goals for your organization or team. Put these goals in writing and give copies to each member of the group.

Variations:
The format used in this exercise has a multitude of uses. Use this process or variations of it any time you need input from the group.

SETTING INDIVIDUAL GOALS
Goals:
● To involve the individual follower in setting personal goals.
● To identify what the leader will need to do to serve the individual as he or she works toward his or her personal goals.
● To build trust and open communication between the leader and the follower.

Group size:
One person at a time.

Time required:
About 1 hour for the first meeting, with additional sessions as needed.

Materials needed:
   Blank sheets of paper
   Pens or pencils
   2 file folders

Procedure:
   1. Open the discussion of personal goals by reassuring the follower of your confidence in his or her ability. Review your team's goals and point out how these goals cannot be achieved unless each team member has a personal set of goals that meet some aspect of the team's goals. Discuss the follower's role in reaching the overall team goals. Ask the follower to share his or her views on what his or her personal contribution should be, making sure that the goals are discussed in terms of exactly *what* the follower will do, *how much* the follower will do, and *by when* it will be completed. When you and the follower have agreed on goals, write them down, and have your follower write them down as well.
   2. Discuss with the follower how you can serve his or her needs as he or she works toward the goals. Once again, these responsibilities should be written down by both of you. Remember to state them in terms of *what, how much,* and *by when.*
   3. Place the sheets of paper in file folders marked with the follower's name. Set a time to get together with the follower to review his or her progress in reaching the goals.

Variations:
   The leader can also use this format when setting goals with small groups or teams working together on a specific project.

EVALUATING INDIVIDUAL PERFORMANCE
Goals:
   ● To evaluate the follower's progress toward reaching personal goals.

• To evaluate the leader's performance as he or she serves the follower's needs in accomplishing his or her goals.
• To develop and maintain trust and open communication between the follower and the leader.
• To help the leader and follower evaluate the follower's progress in developing leadership skills.

Group size:
One person at a time.

Time required:
30 minutes to 1 hour (or as much time as needed).

Materials needed:
Blank sheets of paper
Pens or pencils
Completed personal goals sheets for both the follower and the leader

Procedure:
1. Begin the discussion by evaluating how well you as leader have done in meeting the needs of the follower as he or she has worked on accomplishing the personal goals you set together. Ask for honest input from the follower. Record any unmet needs on both sheets of paper (the leader's and the follower's). Decide together how you will meet those needs.

2. Evaluate the follower's progress and record any corrective action needed on both sheets of paper.

3. Evaluate the follower's work as it relates to developing leadership skills. Determine with the follower what actions need to be taken in order for the follower to begin moving through the five steps of leadership development described in chapter 11 of this book. Record these actions and decisions on both sheets of paper.

4. Set a time to get together with the follower to continue evaluating his or her performance. Use this process in future

meetings.

Variations:
You can also use this format when evaluating performance of small groups working on specialized projects.

SETTING LIMITS ON DECISION-MAKING POWER
Goals:
● To determine both the follower's and leader's limits of decision-making power as a follower works toward accomplishing a specific project.
● To help both the follower and leader develop greater understanding of the follower's responsibilities for the project.

Group size:
One person at a time.

Time required:
Approximately 15–30 minutes for each task.

Materials needed:
Blank sheets of paper
Pens or pencils
Folders containing the goals and tasks being evaluated

Procedure:
1. At any time the need arises, discuss with the follower the amount of decision-making power the follower will have as he or she works on his or her assignment. Discuss the type of input each of you will need from the other as you make your decisions and determine how and when that input will be given.
2. Record your decisions in each person's folder. These guidelines will play a part in the ongoing performance evaluation process.

Variations:
This process can also be used for setting decision-making limits for small groups working on specialized projects.

DEMONSTRATING THE ROLE OF COMMUNICATION IN GROUP PRODUCTIVITY

Goals:
● To demonstrate the effect of communication on productivity.
● To show that some forms of communication aid productivity more than others.
● To illustrate the emotional effects of poor communication on leaders and followers.

Group size:
Ten or more people.

Time required:
45–60 minutes

Physical setting:
A meeting space large enough for the group to sit in rows of chairs facing a chalkboard or flip chart. There will also need to be space for the group to break up into small groups of 3–6 people each to work on small-group assignments. There must also be a space available outside the meeting room, but close by, where you can send 3 pairs of people. It is very important that the people in this area not be able to see or hear what is going on in the meeting room during the exercise.

Materials needed:
Ruler
Marking pen or chalk
Copy of the drawing shown for each group member
Pencil and paper for each group member

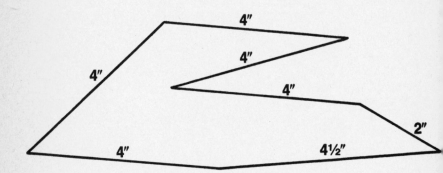

Procedure:

1. Discuss briefly the important role communication plays in a team's productivity.

2. Ask for 6 volunteers. Divide them into pairs and have them leave the room and decide who will be the leader and who will be the follower in each pair. Make sure they won't be able to see or hear you.

3. Distribute copies of the drawing shown to the remaining participants. Explain that you are going to bring the pairs in one at a time. Helped by various forms of communication from the leader, the follower will attempt to draw the figure. Group members should take notes on their observations about how communication influences productivity. Have them conceal their drawings at this time.

4. Call in the first team of 2 people. Have the leader sit in a chair facing the flip chart or chalkboard. The chair should be 10–15 feet away if possible. Give the follower the ruler and marking pen or chalk and explain: the follower is to draw a seven-sided, irregular figure in 2 minutes. He or she may ask the leader any questions about the figure, but the leader may only answer yes or no. Give the leader a copy of the figure to be drawn, making sure the follower does not see the drawing. (You might want to have the drawing in a folder so the follower can't see the image through the paper.) Have them begin.

146

At the end of 2 minutes, show the follower the drawing and have the pair return to their seats. Erase any trace of the work the follower did before the next pair enters.

5. Bring in the next pair. This time have the leader sit in the chair facing *away* from the chalkboard or flip chart. Explain the task as before, with one change: the follower is not permitted to ask the leader any questions or make any sound. He is simply to follow the instructions given by the leader.

After 2 minutes have them return to their seats. Show the follower the diagram, and erase their work.

6. Bring in the last team. Explain the task once again. Once again have the leader sit facing the follower. This time they may communicate in any way they wish. The follower can ask questions, and the leader can give any type of instruction. (He could even show the follower the diagram and say "draw this"—but don't tell the leader he may do that.) Simply explain that they can communicate any way they want to and have 2 minutes for the leader to instruct the follower in drawing the diagram.

After 2 minutes have them stop if they are not finished, and send them back to their chairs.

7. Break the large group up into small groups to discuss their observations on the effects of the different methods of communication. Have the 3 leaders and 3 followers get together and discuss how they felt during the exercise.

8. After 8–10 minutes have the large group reassemble for discussion. List the different modes of communication and how they affect productivity. Have each group member write down how they hope to improve their communication based on what they learned from this exercise.

DEMONSTRATING THE IMPORTANCE OF SERVING
Goals:
- To show the importance of meeting others' needs.
- To demonstrate how a team must focus on the needs of

others in the group in order to effectively accomplish a goal.
● To demonstrate what happens when group members fail
to consider the needs of others.

Group size:
Minimum of 6 people. You will want at least 10 for good
observer feedback. You can have up to 15 observers per
team and as many teams as you wish.

Time required:
Approximately 45 minutes.

Physical setting:
A table and chairs for 6 people, with enough room around
it for up to 15 people to serve as observers.

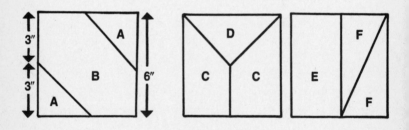

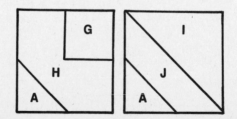

Materials needed:

Pencils

Paper

A set of five envelopes containing pieces of cardboard or heavy paper cut into different patterns which, when properly arranged, will form five squares of equal size. To prepare a set, cut out five cardboard squares, each exactly 6″ x 6″. Place the squares in a row and mark them as shown in the diagram on page 148, penciling in the letters lightly so they can be erased. The lines should be drawn so that when the pieces are cut out, pieces marked with the same letter will be the same size. Cut each square along the lines shown in the diagram to make the parts of the puzzle. Number the five envelopes, and distribute the cardboard pieces as follows:

Envelope 1: pieces I, H, and E

Envelope 2: pieces A, A, A, and C

Envelope 3: pieces A and J

Envelope 4: pieces D and F

Envelope 5: pieces G, B, F, and C

Erase the penciled letters from the pieces and write instead their envelope numbers. This makes it easy to return the pieces to the proper envelopes for use with other groups. Or each set could be made from a different color of cardboard or paper.[1]

Procedure:

1. You will need six volunteers for each team. Have each team elect one of their members to serve as judge for the group. The six volunteers should sit around a table, and the remaining people should gather around the table. Distribute the five envelopes to the five volunteers seated at the table. (The judge does not get an envelope.)

1. The drawings for this exercise were reproduced by permission from *A Handbook of Structured Experiences for Human Relations Training, Volume I,* J. William Pfeiffer and John E. Jones, Editors. LaJolla: University Associates Publishers, Inc., 1974.

Give the team the following instructions: Each of you has an envelope containing pieces of paper for forming a square. Your task is to form 5 squares of equal size. The project will not be completed until each team member has a perfect square of the same size as those in front of the other team members. While working on this project, there is to be no talking, pointing, or any other form of communication. People may offer pieces to others, but they can't reach out and take pieces unless they are offered. People can't place their pieces in the center for others to take. It is permissible for a person to give away all of his pieces. The judge is responsible for strictly enforcing these rules.

The observers should look for the following:

Who is willing to give away pieces to help others?

Does anyone finish his puzzle and then withdraw from the group effort?

Are there people unwilling to give away their pieces, even when theirs don't fit?

What is the level of frustration and why?

Is there a point after which the group cooperates better?

Do people violate the rules? If so, how does the judge handle it?

2. At the end of the project have the group discuss what they observed and learned about the importance of meeting others' needs. Have group members write out a personal application of what they learned in the exercise.

CLARIFYING FOLLOWERS' ROLES
Goals:
● To generate better communication between the leader and the follower.
● To clarify the roles the follower and leader will assume as the follower progresses toward becoming a leader.
● To clarify the levels of decision-making responsibility the leader and follower will assume as the follower progresses toward becoming a leader.

Time required:
Clarifying the role between a leader and one follower may take 2–3 hours. If it is a larger group it may take 2–3 days, depending on the number of people involved.

Materials needed:
Pencils
Paper
Several pieces of newsprint
Marking pens
Masking tape

Procedure:
1. Meet with the follower (or group) and explain the purpose and goals of the exercise.
2. Have the follower write out his or her fears and expectations for the exercise. Discuss them together.
3. Have the follower write on newsprint the role the leader should assume with the follower as the follower works on his or her assigned project. At the same time the leader, on a separate sheet of newsprint, defines his or her role as he or she sees it. The areas covered should include duties, areas of responsibility, and amount of decision-making power.
4. Post the completed sheets of newsprint. Review the follower's input and compare it with yours and negotiate your actual role until the two of you reach an agreement. Once the leader's role has been negotiated, use the same process to negotiate the follower's role.

This process should be used each time the follower moves to a different level of leadership as described in chapter 11 of this book.

COMPARING PERSONAL GOALS WITH TEAM GOALS
Goals:
● To understand the follower's personal goals as they compare with the team's goals.

● To help the follower determine whether his or her personal goals and priorities are compatible with those of the team.

● To determine how the follower's goals can be achieved by accomplishing the team's goals.

Group size:
One person at a time or small groups of no more than 10.

Time required:
30–60 minutes, depending on the size of the group.

Materials needed:
Paper and pencil for each person
A chalkboard or flip chart
Chalk or marking pen

Procedure:
1. Take a few minutes to introduce the exercise by talking about the importance of personal and team goals and the need for the team's goals to be rewarding and motivational to the follower.

2. Have the follower write on a piece of paper his personal goals and priorities for his life. Meanwhile, write out the goals and priorities of the team.

3. When both are ready, have the follower write his or her goals on the chalkboard or flip chart. Then write the team's goals beside the follower's and together discuss the compatibility of the follower's goals with the team's goals. If the follower's goals are not compatible with the team's goals, discuss whether they can be or not. If not, help the follower find a group or team that will be more compatible with his or her personal goals.

If the follower's goals are compatible with the team's goals, identify skills the follower has that can be effectively used in achieving the team's goals and determine how those skills will best be used.

DEVELOPING PLANNING SKILLS
Goals:
- To develop effective planning skills on the part of followers.
- To teach the need for delegation in the planning process.
- To teach the need for attention to details in the planning process.
- To identify people who assume leadership responsibilities during the planning process.

Group size:
    3–6 people per team, any number of teams

Time required:
    45–60 minutes

Physical setting:
    A room large enough for a table with chairs for each group or team participating.

Materials needed:
    Paper and pencil for each group
    Flip chart and marking pen or chalkboard and chalk
    Newsprint and masking tape

Procedure:
    1. Give each group this assignment: You are to plan a family picnic to be held in 6 months, on July 4. There will be a family of four coming from each of the 50 states. Your job is to completely plan the picnic on paper. You must consider such things as activities during the picnic, invitations, who will be responsible for what, target dates for each phase of the planning from now to the day of the picnic, how expenses will be covered, and so on. Write out your plan on sheets of newsprint, showing the time of each activity in the plan, who will be responsible for it, and so forth. When you are finished, post your completed plan on the wall.

As each team works on this assignment the leader should circulate from team to team, watching for the following:
● How quickly does each team get organized to work on the plan?
● Who emerges as the leader of the team and how does that happen?
● How much attention to detail do they give the plan?
● How well does the group work together?
● Do they leave out or overlook major parts of the plan?
● How willing are people to serve one another?
2. After each group posts its completed plan, discuss with the group what they learned about the planning process. Refer to what you observed while the work was being done. At the end of the discussion, list the planning principles that were illustrated by the exercise and have each follower identify in writing how he or she will more effectively apply those principles.

HELPING FOLLOWERS IDENTIFY THEIR PRIORITIES
Goals:
● To help followers clearly understand their priorities.
● To help followers determine whether their priorities need to be changed.
● To help followers make any needed changes in their priorities.

Time required:
30 minutes

Materials needed:
Paper
Pencils
Chalkboard and chalk or flip chart and marking pen

Procedure:
1. Spend a few minutes explaining the importance of

clearly understanding our priorities in life.

Give blank sheets of paper to group members and have them tear the sheets in half. Have them then tear the two halves in thirds so that they wind up with 6 small pieces of paper of equal size. Have them write out the six most important priorities in their lives, one for each piece of paper.

Then tell them to discard the least important of the 6 priorities, then another, and another, until they have only one priority left. This represents their most important priority.

2. Have group members decide whether they are satisfied with their priorities and their order of importance. If not, have them work on resetting their priorities.

Variations:

You may want to assign the task of comparing participants' priorities with what the Bible says our priorities should be. If theirs are different from the Bible's priorities, such as those found in Luke 9:23 and Matthew 6:33, ask them to spend time alone with God seeking His direction concerning what their priorities should be.